MY HUSBAND WEARS MY CLOTHES

MY HUSBAND WEARS MY CLOTHES

Crossdressing from the
Perspective of a Wife

by
Peggy J. Rudd, Ed.D.

PM PUBLISHERS
Katy, Texas

Published 1999 by PM Publishers

Publisher's Cataloging-in-Publication
(Provided by Quality Books, Inc.)

Rudd, Peggy J.
    My husband wears my clothes: crossdressing from the
perspective of a wife / by Peggy J. Rudd - 2nd ed
    P.cm

    Includes bibliographical references and index
    Preassigned LCCN: 98-067950
    ISBN: 0-9626762-5-X

    1. Transvestism. 2. Transvestites. 3. Transvestites-
Family relationships I. Title

HQ77.8.R83R83 1999   306.77
                             QBI98-1269

Printed in the United States of America

CONTENTS

vi

ACKNOWLEDGMENTS

I wish to express my thanks to the members of TAU CHI, the Houston Chapter of TRI ESS, for their loving support and editorial assistance.

I am very grateful to Carol Beecroft and Virginia Prince who shared my dream for this first book written from the perspective of the crossdresser's wife. Virginia spent many hours of her precious time editing the original copy on her word processor. Carol, in turn, distributed this copy nationally as a preliminary field test. I appreciate their many years of leadership and their friendship to me personally.

Most of all I wish to thank Melanie, my husband, who taught me that crossdressing can be a beautiful word.

This book is dedicated to readers who are seeking truth about crossdressing. By reading this book you are demonstrating a desire to understand this complex phenomenon.

INTRODUCTION

For a number of years, I have been married to a crossdresser, a man who enjoys wearing women's clothing. In the case of my husband it is frequently my clothing that is worn. Does that seem strange to you? I must admit that it was difficult for me to comprehend this most unusual practice. There was a time when I wished that some morning I would wake up and the whole crossdressing situation would be gone forever.

Today the expression, "Clothes don't make the man," has a new meaning for us. My husband is as loveable in my clothes as in his. In fact he seems to be a more complete person when the feminine side of his personality is openly expressed by wearing feminine clothes. For me acceptance and understanding have been accomplished by reading, interacting with others who crossdress, and being sensitive to my husband and his needs.

I have had a strong desire to share our story: the struggles and the triumphs. We feel that this information will be of special interest to wives, girl friends, family members and friends of crossdressers. Helping them move toward understanding and acceptance is my goal. Crossdressers, as a group, are capable of being excellent husbands, fathers, sons and friends. The relationship my husband and I share has proven this, but it has not always been easy. My husband, like most crossdressers, did not fully understand the situation himself. Because of the lack of understanding of his own personality, particularly of his feminine side, he could not communicate his needs to me. In time we overcame the negatives, and we believe others can also. To change the negatives into positives will require flexibility in preconceived ideas on femininity and masculinity, and compromise from all persons involved.

There are both positive and negative ways to come to an understanding of crossdressing. In most cases when the wife cannot accept her husband's need to express his feminine side, there could be problems relating to how she discovered her husband's femmeself. Many crossdressers make the mistake of introducing their wives to crossdressing by taking them to a show where female impersonators are featured. The female impersonators usually present the illusion of being beautiful women, but the wife may object to the atmosphere and the frequent references to homosexuality. She may immediately relate crossdressing to homosexuality and begin to fear that her husband is gay. The prospects of her coming to an understanding may be reduced.

My introduction to Melanie, the name chosen for my husband's feminine side, came in the form of an article written by my husband and a letter written one month after we were married. Our love and commitment were very secure at the time. The letter my husband had written expressed his love for me. At the same time it gave me the background needed to pave the way toward understanding and acceptance of his need to crossdress. My first response was not automatically positive. Over the coming days and weeks, however, I grew to the point of feeling that, "Life can go on, even with Melanie in our home."

Today we feel that our relationship is stronger because Melanie exists. Femininity adds a nice ingredient to my husband's personality. In general we feel the world would be a better place if there could be less machismo, and a better balance of human personalities. Our hope is that others will be able to understand and accept crossdressing as we do.

Crossdressing is compatible with a happy and stable marriage if there is love and commitment to each other and a commitment to the relationship. An open honesty before marriage is probably the best way to handle this delicate situation for most couples, but I can not say what would have happened if I had been told before marriage. It is possible that I would have walked away from the greatest love of my life. This love is portrayed in a poem composed before being introduced to Melanie, my husband's feminine side.

One day millions of years ago,
There was a plan for your life and mine;
Somewhere, sometimes our hearts
Were destined to intertwine.
Time passed slowly while we waited,
But hope lingered all the while;
Then one day I found you,
And now I smile!

In moments of retrospection we remember our first meeting. We were two singles living in a small town near Houston, Texas. My husband was interested in our local single's group and the organization's plan to attend a state convention in San Antonio. This is what brought him to my front door one January evening in 1980.

We both recall the instant compatibility and conversational ease as we sat in my living room planning the trip. Later that night I became the woman in my husband's dream fantasy. He dreamed that I loved and accepted him dressed as a woman.

Two weeks later we boarded a van heading for San Antonio. At the convention we laughed, talked, heard inspirational speeches, and walked the beautiful meandering river that runs through this historic city. The following October we were married in an elegant yet simple ceremony.

Soon thereafter I was introduced to Melanie, the feminine side of my husband's personality. Melanie and I have captured the joys of two people in love. We consider each moment special gift. Together at the close of each day as we watch the crimson rays of sun color the blazing Texas sky, we're thankful for life and the experiences we share together including crossdressing.

Many times I have pondered the circumstances that brought us to this point. Convinced that an understanding of the sociological, etiological, and emotional implications of crossdressing could help others, I committed myself to the completion of this book.

The words you read here come from a review of the literature on crossdressing, from a vast array of friendships with cross-dressers, from shared experiences with other wives and family members of crossdressers and from many hours of counseling with these persons. Most of all it comes from the heart. I hope that each reader will find the truth as we have experienced it.

The purpose of this book is to make factual, helpful information available in a unique area of the behavioral sciences. The intended result should be an understanding of this very complex phenomenon and an acceptance of crossdressers. Objections that have been expressed by wives and family members of crossdressers are addressed. Experiences of others who have solved their problems will be passed on so that those who are still contending with the many complex issues can be helped. This book will serve as a guide and a source book for students and professionals in the behavioral sciences and family members or friends of crossdressers. It may even help the crossdresser himself crystallize his true identity.

In writing this book I am not exalting or advocating crossdressing. My purpose is to help eliminate many of the misconceptions. Society has been repressive. This is because people do not understand the true feelings and behavioral patterns of crossdressers. What people do not understand, they tend to fear, and fear breeds prejudice. As the reader grows in awareness my hope is that tolerance and understanding will grow proportionately. I do not expect readers to accept all of my thoughts and theories, but I do hope that this subject can be approached with an open mind.

CHAPTER ONE

A WIFE'S INTRODUCTION TO CROSSDRESSING

I remember well my first in-depth understanding of the word "transvestite." It was on an autumn day in early November and the crispness of fall was in the air. I was a happy bride who had just received roses to commemorate the first month of marriage. On that November day, my husband surprised me with a brief visit to the office where I was involved in the mundane tasks expected of an administrator. His visit provided a welcome diversion from the usual set of activities including dealing with people in my office and doing paper work.

After a few moments together, he started toward the door. "Here, honey," he said, "I want you to read this journal article." The article, written several years before by my husband, was about counseling conducted with a transvestite and his wife as a part of my husband's work in a Veterans Administration Hospital.

I read the article eagerly and felt pride because the article was a well-written literary effort. In my search for "Mr. Right" there was a secret desire to fall in love with a man who could share my interest in literary pursuits and a man who was intelligent and conversant on many subjects. This article seemed to be a dramatic demonstration of his diversified knowledge.

"Transvestite" ... I muttered the word to myself again. I had only a surface awareness of this word and its meaning. Walking into the outer office where two of my secretaries were sitting, I spoke the word more audibly. "Transvestite. What does that mean to you?" One secretary did not respond. She looked at me with an empty expression. The other shrugged her shoulders and replied,

"Oh, you know, that's one of those men who always want to wear women's clothing."

With that statement, she had just verbalized the extent of my own shallow understanding. Because my husband had been involved as a therapist with transvestites, and because he had written the journal article on the subject, I felt compelled to learn more. This is one characteristic of contented, secure, newlywed couples. They hunger to close the gaps of their two lives through understanding and want to be one in all aspects of life.

DEFINITIONS OF TRANSVESTISM

Perhaps I did not want my husband to know how little I knew about the subject. It could be that I was only curious, or maybe it was the joy of wedded bliss that motivated me to learn more. That evening I found several books in our home library written on the subject of transvestism. In the book TRANSVESTITES AND TRANSSEXUALS by Debora Feinbloom, there was a clear definition. "A **transvestite** is a person who crossdresses. Anyone who wears clothing that is usually associated with the opposite sex could be called a transvestite." This definition forced me to consider myself a transvestite when masculine clothing fits the mood or need in my own life. The word **transvestite** stirred a negative connotation. Almost from the first I preferred the word **crossdresser,** since this word described the actions more clearly.

Virginia Prince, a crossdresser who lives her life as a woman, wrote a similar definition but added a new synonym, femmophile. According to Prince,

Transvestism or femmophilia is a form of behavior and personality expression characterized by a desire to wear the clothing of the opposite gender. The word comes from the Latin, i.e. Trans, meaning across, and Vesta, meaning clothing. Therefore the word literally means crossdressing.

Since the term **Transvestism** is applied indiscriminately to all who crossdress without regard to their motives or purposes, the terms **Femmophilia** for the condition and **Femmophile** for the individual have been coined. These terms mean love of the feminine and are applied to persons whose interest is solely in the feminine gender role without a sexual connotation.

Soon it became evident that crossdressing is not a new phenomenon. Chevalier d'Eon, a nobleman in the court of Louis XV of France, dressed as a woman while he carried out diplomatic missions. Transvestism is sometimes called **Eonism** in honor of d'Eon. At this time I knew a little more about what a transvestite is and also felt glad that the words crossdresser, femmophile, or eonism could be substituted for the word that I disliked, transvestite.

ARE CROSSDRESSERS GAY?

There were still big gaps in my understanding. For one thing I realized that homosexual queens also dress as women. I pondered the difference between that type of crossdressing and that of femmophiles. It was becoming apparent to me that the latter have no intention of acting out sexually with other men. They have a love for women and are attracted to them because of the softness, beauty and charm which they personify. I came to understand that in many ways crossdressing for the transvestite is an external, visible, conscious manifestation of an internal, subconscious, feminine feeling. Crossdressers are secretive, largely because they have not been able to crash through the preconceived ideas of society that tend to stereotype people as distinctly masculine or feminine.

WHY DO SOME CROSSDRESSERS ACT MACHO?

In an effort to disguise the strong feminine feelings from within, many crossdressers inadvertently become "macho." They try very hard to convince the world and themselves they are "normal." "Macho" is a disguise behind which they can safely hide. Such a disguise became a lifestyle for Beth, a crossdresser from Oklahoma, who writes,

> Since I started dressing at ten years of age, I would act as macho as possible and always put up this unfeeling, insensitive front. It has hardened me to where I cannot express much sensitivity or show feelings like I would want to. Even when I receive gifts from my family on my birthday or Christmas I can't show what I feel in my heart. I have trained myself to do the opposite. I probably put up more of a macho front than the average man, but I believe I am more in tune with women than the average man. I appreciate them more, especially their efforts to look good. Despite what others may think I am not sick, diseased, or strange. I want to live my life as a male part of the time and as a female at other times. I want peace and harmony in my life and with others. This has not always been possible.

> As a child my father caught me crossdressed a few times. Once in anger he broke my nose. The next day I crossdressed again. To me crossdressing is like enjoying the forbidden fruit. I have been embarrassed, beaten, and humiliated in front of other people. They called me "naughty" and mentally ill because I dressed as a girl. In spite of the embarrassment, I still crossdressed with vigor every opportunity I had. Sometimes there are stages when I don't like myself, but this is usually related to my appearance and weight. This feeling is the only deterring force that works to keep me from crossdressing. I go through a phase of self-improvements and then the urge to crossdress occurs again.

Beth's story is a perfect example of the "macho" trap. Many crossdressers state that if they ever decide to have psychotherapy it would be to help them defeat the inhibitions that keep the feminine side hidden. They do not want a "cure" for crossdressing. They enjoy their femininity. In order to defend the sensitive personality traits from societal condemnation many crossdressers adopt a less appropriate "macho" veneer.

Further reading revealed that many crossdressers have known the agony of not being understood and accepted. They keep the secret of their feminine side to themselves because they do not want to be rejected. Meanwhile they continue acting the role society has assigned to them as men. Some of them find pleasure in that role, but they can use feminine clothing to express the true feelings, moods, and personality which has a very strong feminine side.

ARE WOMEN SOMETIMES CROSSDRESSERS?

In a broader sense, I came to understand that crossdressers are persons, male or female, who enjoy wearing the clothing of the opposite gender. Since women in our culture can wear men's clothing almost without impunity, the term **crossdresser** usually refers to men who have an exaggerated liking for femininity. They gain emotional satisfaction from wearing clothing appropriate to women in our culture.

The pattern and extent of crossdressing varies among crossdressers. One group of crossdressers may wear women's apparel only periodically, such as on Halloween or during Mardigras. Other crossdressers may have a fondness for one or several articles of clothing, e.g., panties or a brassiere, which may be worn occasionally or habitually under their masculine clothing. For a small number of crossdressers the need to crossdress and express femininity may lead them to discard all male clothing. They embark upon a life long expression of femininity and want to be perceived as women. These people are **transgenderists**.

THE SEARCH FOR TRUTH
AND UNDERSTANDING

After several weeks of reading and study, I had reached a clinical awareness of crossdressing. In the days that followed I came to understand the human side of this complex phenomenon. I had become so interested in learning terminology that I almost failed to recognize the purpose of my introduction to the world of crossdressing by my husband. When I finally put the books down long enough to look into my husband's eyes, I saw a great amount of pain and anxiety. I observed that he had become tense and was having difficulty sleeping at night. He appeared to be on the brink of shattering at the most gentle touch. I encouraged him to discuss this problem openly. He then told me that there was a part of his personality that he had not shared with me. He said, "There is a part of me that is out of step with society. I love you and I don't want to lose you because of it. I am afraid to tell you, but I want us to be honest."

During the next several days I examined our love. Realizing that our relationship had brought us to the heights of ecstacy never before experienced, I felt compelled to express my love and commitment once again. Lying in bed late one night I whispered to him, "Darling, please feel confident of my love. Regardless of what it is that is hurting you at this moment, our love is bigger. There is no problem we cannot resolve together."

The next day my husband visited my office and presented me with an epistle titled, "My Ultimate Fantasy." The thirty page letter described his life as a crossdresser, the agony related to his dual life, and his fantasy of me accepting him fully dressed as a woman.

During the next several months I searched for truth and understanding. I came to the conclusion that my husband is the most precious person I have ever known. Perhaps this fact has led me through the paths of agony, fear and loneliness to victory. My understanding and acceptance was not an automatic positive response to what was initially a negative stimulus. There have been many times when I wished for an escape from the entire situation. With the help of my husband I have reached my present level. I love Melanie and know she is a part of Mel. I would not exchange my life with anyone. My husband and I have shared a kaleidoscope of joy as lovers, sisters, best friends, confidants, and companions. We are fortunate to have each other. I would like to share our formula for a happy marriage. Perhaps these ideas will help others who are experiencing a marriage that includes crossdressing. The formula includes these things:

WE CONTINUE TO GROW

A wise man once said that if a person stops growing he has stopped living. This statement could also be applied to human interactions, and especially the marital relationship. When a marriage becomes stagnant it is no longer alive. Couples should constantly search for ways to improve and grow. Many couples complain that love has gone out of their marriage and there is no zest and excitement remaining in the relationship. The couple that continues to grow will say their relationship becomes more secure and solid each day. There is continual growth in understanding, patience and empathy. Each day brings them to new heights.

My husband and I have continued to grow in our marriage and believe the best is yet to come. We will be students in the art of marriage for the rest of our lives. The crossdresser and his wife have dimensions of their relationship that are unique. These include the mutual sharing of wardrobe planning, makeup, image fashioning, color analysis, the arts, cooking, sewing and girl talk. These offer growth opportunities.

As I have grown in my understanding of Melanie, my husband has grown in his understanding of himself. Most negative feelings were replaced with positive ones. I believe I am a better person because I am married to a crossdresser. I felt rewarded when my husband's needs became a top priority in my life, because I gained a confidence in our relationship that might never have existed. It should be said, however, that while it is important to give my husband's needs a top priority, my own needs can not be neglected. It is much easier to give to another when your own needs have been met. Too many crossdressers want to have their own needs met while their wives' needs are ignored. Then they wonder why wives reject their crossdressing.

For years my husband suppressed the desire to crossdress. If he attempted to express femininity there was resistance from his family and society. Today I feel satisfaction when I see my husband's femininity vibrantly expressed. Our house is more than a building made of brick. Ours is a home where Melanie can be herself without fear of rejection, embarrassment or condemnation. Melanie is a definite part of my husband's personality that must be expressed. In our home my husband will never be treated as abnormal because of his crossdressing.

WE KEEP THE COURTSHIP ALIVE

The problem with many marriages is that courtship is left at the altar. I believe a couple's courtship should continue throughout life. For this to become reality both husband and wife must be committed to the idea that life is an adventure. Regardless of daily pressures, work loads, or demands by children or other family members, there must be time allocated in the day for both to work together to develop the love relationship. This is the foundation of courtship, the discovery of each other and the sharing of joys that you both deserve.

My husband and I enjoy going out frequently for dinner in a nice restaurant and attending the theatre. Other couples have their own favorite activities. The types of courtship activities are irrelevant as long as both find pleasure in them. The wives of crossdressers seem to have an even greater need for romantic activities. The wife gives up a part of the courtship time to share in feminine activities with her husband. He must be very careful to let her be courted by his masculine side. One wife remarked to me recently, "I have needs too. Why doesn't someone think of my needs?" The husband who ignores the needs of his wife is not demonstrating that he cares about her. Such a demonstration would help the wife to feel inclined to accept her husband's crossdressing. Some femmophiles have trouble with this. Could it be the macho trap again? Or could it be a preoccupation with their own gender conflict?

One way to keep the courtship alive is through good grooming. There is nothing that dilutes sexual attraction faster than teeth that are not brushed or a body that is not clean. I have seen some crossdressers who are aware of current feminine grooming trends and take a lot of time in their feminine appearance but disregard their masculine grooming. This becomes a turn off for the wife who then begins to resist any acceptance of her husband's need to crossdress. The wife wants to share life with an attractive man who is well groomed, not just with a well groomed woman. Many crossdressers believe the two personalities are separate. They are not. The husband needs to reinforce that he is satisfied being a man and with his own masculinity. Otherwise the wife will remind him that, "I married a man not a woman."

WE ARE SUPPORTIVE OF EACH OTHER

During the time we have been married I have felt the "pain" experienced by my husband because he is a crossdresser. The pain was caused by family members who could not understand or accept my husband's need to express the feminine side of his personality. When this has happened I have tried to be supportive of him. I did not attempt to retaliate against these family members; rather, I would defend my husband with words based on my own understanding of crossdressing. Patiently I have tried to lead others, especially other family members, to understanding and acceptance. I have found that when people understand they tend to be less judgmental .

WE TRY TO UNDERSTAND

All people have idiosyncracies and differences in their personalities. Our agreement has always been that we will try to understand these differences. I have described the beauty of our love and relationship. This is a reality. Another reality is that things will not always be perfect. When the going gets tough we are committed to trying harder than ever to understand. Understanding is a two way street.

Many wives of crossdressers feel that their husbands don't understand the complexity of their emotions either. Although it is important that she understand her husband's needs, neglecting her own needs can be very dangerous. She may need to first crystalize what those needs are, understand them herself, and then help her husband understand them. Understanding must be a partner with compromise. The important thing is that she becomes committed to a dynamic relationship.

WE KEEP THE LINES OF COMMUNICATION OPEN

If you are the wife of a crossdresser you probably have some underlying fears. My husband and I openly discuss the fears that I previously experienced. Every aspect of transvestism has been openly discussed. My husband has patiently explained his theories on crossdressing. We have studied extensively on the subject. Putting prejudices aside, we have tried to be logical and intelligent in our communication.

The formula for a happy marriage presented here has worked for us. Perhaps as you read this book you will be able to design your own plan. With open communication you will be able to formulate ideas that will fit your own unique situation. Communicate with your wife or husband. Share ideas and dreams.

A sign hangs on one wall of our home that states,

Accept me as I am.
Only then can we begin
to accept each other.

CHAPTER TWO

LIBERATION OF THE TOTAL PERSON

Recently during a very long and emotional conversation with Susan, the wife of a crossdresser, she shared her deepest feelings. "I truly love Tom," she said, with a tremor in her voice. "I have always cared for him. Why else would I be around after 30 years? But I find crossdressing very difficult to accept even after all this time. It seems to go against everything I was ever taught about human nature. Please help me understand," she pleaded.

Why did Susan have difficulty accepting her husband's crossdressing? This warm, loving woman was exerting every ounce of effort to come to grips with a problem that seemed bigger than her ability to cope. A great "force" seemed to pull her away from the mental attitude needed to accept the fact that her husband was a crossdresser.

What is that force? I believe it is the result of years of conditioning in a tightly crystallized formula for what women do, what men do, with no space for deviation from the established formula. It is the solid development of an attitude about how life should be lived. Susan had been conforming to society's dictates since she was a child. Now this conformity was creating problems as she tried to live in a grown-up world. Sometimes it appears that the two gender roles seldom share a common ground.

What is the source of this force? It comes from the minds of people, millions of them, a society. It comes from history. It comes from tradition. Since much of our difficulty in accepting crossdressing has its roots in these traditions and mores, we should look more closely at them. As children we quoted this nursery rhyme and believed it:

> **Sugar and spice and everything nice**
> **that's what little girls are made of!**
> **Frogs and snails and puppy dog tails**
> **that's what little boys are made of!**

In spite of sweeping social changes during this century, society dictates that the two recipes for gender must stay the same. This nursery rhyme spells out clearly the parameters for each gender. For years society has expected men, women, boys and girls to perform according to preconceived role expectations that appear to be set in concrete. Sometimes it seems that the "twain" between these two distinctly different role expectations will never share any common ground. Indeed the recipes tend to be set down in a cookbook of stone.

Girls are expected to be what the nursery rhyme calls, "everything nice." In every word, thought and deed, they must be kind, loving, gentle and giving. For many years girls were expected to live out their lives to fulfill the paramount goal of being blue ribbon wives and mothers. Ideally each women was to wear a ruffled, white apron, love cooking and sewing, and know the art of keeping quiet in public. They were so passive and submissive that in many cases they had no unique identity except as the wives of particular men.

THE NEW FEMALE IMAGE

During recent times we have seen the evolution of a **new female image.** Psychologists recognize that women are complex beings, capable of reaching beyond their previous roles as traditional homemakers. Women changed from the corseted lady of the 18th century to the emancipated women of today. The most telling change initiated was probably the introduction of large numbers of women into the work force during World War II. After tasting that independence and new interest, they were reluctant to return to traditional roles.

The dictates of clothing correspond directly with the spoken and unspoken wishes of these women to imitate men. Current fashion trends enable latent fetish tendencies to work themselves out within the social framework of acceptable behavior. These fashions are directed toward the creation of the "phallic woman." The boat and leather fetishism, masquerading under the guise of fashion, sheds light on the underlying psychodynamics of the new, more complex woman. Women are demonstrating with clothing that they feel liberated from preconceived expectations. Women are seen today in business suits, and the dress for success seems to imitate masculine fashion.

These changes in gender identity have occurred faster than society has been willing to assimilate. There are some negative reactions to the new female image. Many times the women who have become assertive and aggressive are looked upon with an element of distrust, while the conservative, traditional woman is greatly admired. The admirers are looking for a reflection of the "good old days" when Grandma made homemade bread and churned her own butter. To encourage the continuation of stereotyped female roles, little girls are actively taught femininity. They are given dolls for Christmas, treated with gentle kindness, and led into the world of "sugar and spice and everything nice." While these stereotypes are not adhered to by all families, this has become the norm and most of us are affected by it.

MASCULINE GENDER EXPECTATIONS

The little boys in the same family may be given army trucks and boxing gloves as a forerunner to their future roles as protectors of society. Parents teach their sons to be tough and to avoid feminine traits. They must never cry or show emotion because this behavior is not "manly." To further lock the child into masculine gender expectations a father will teach his son to play aggressive games. Thus it seems boys are forced into the world of macho at a very early age. By the time a boy is five years old he dreams of being a big man like his father. He wishes for hair on his chest and may be caught with a magnifying glass checking to see if any hair is growing on his body. By age twelve he has practiced making his voice deeper and has felt a terrific embarrassment and frustration when his voice breaks into high soprano.

Meanwhile many parents continue to use every opportunity to teach their sons to be dominant and assertive. Boys are taught to prefer blue over pink and tailored over ruffled. They are even taught to prefer meat and potatoes over dainty party food. Real men don't eat quiche. With these external stimuli feeding the development of their masculine identity, they now begin the climb toward success.

Fortunately for the crossdresser these examples are somewhat exaggerated and social attitudes have begun to change. Some families may give a truck to a little girl and a doll to the little brother. Most parents no longer subscribe so drastically to the societal stereotypes. Even parents that would be uncomfortable with their sons playing with dolls are more open to personality variations. These changes have helped families of crossdressers accept him enfemme.

MEN AND WOMEN, IS THERE A DIFFERENCE?

Some experts have been taking a second look at these stereotyped roles just described. Social scientists are saying that while culture and society have dictated major differences between the genders, such differences are in fact minimal. One such expert, Bill Simon, Professor of Sociology, The University of Houston, asserted that there are only three basic differences between men

and women:
1) **Males have the capacity to impregnate.**
2) **Females have the capacity to be impregnated, and**
3) **Females have the capacity to lactate.**

Recent discoveries in the field of genetics also shed some light. An excellent example is the book, "Brain Sex" by Ann Moire.

Even Dr. Simon's list can be debated. For example, some men, because of low sperm count, can't impregnate. Physiological factors may prevent a woman's pregnancy, or she may prefer artificial insemination. Males can lactate when given the proper hormones. Women lactate following giving birth because their bodies produce that hormone. It is the hormone that causes lactation.

In a telephone interview with Dr. Simon, it became clear that many sociologists now perceive the human behavior of men and women to be overlapping. The lines of separation between the roles of men and women have begun to dissolve. The Simon theory has been documented by sociological and anthropological writings. In her book, MALE AND FEMALE, Margaret Mead asserted that apart from reproduction and basic sex differences there is no difference between men and women. This concept is not new. Over one hundred years ago George Band remarked that society tends to overestimate the differences between sexes. This theory has been accelerated in recent years. With their ruffled aprons tucked away in drawers, women have taken their places beside men in the working world. This has erased some of the lines previously drawn between the sexes. It is not unusual today to see women police officers, wallpaper hangers, doctors and engineers. What may be a feminine occupation in recent western society's view, may be a masculine job in some other society and vice versa. Previously careers were also controlled by society and environmental conditioning. Boys became engineers because they supposedly possessed higher aptitudes in mathematics and spatial judgments. The unanswered questions, however, are to what degree is this superiority inborn, and how have expectations molded these skills? Girls on the other hand tend to be more literary and are expected to be comfortable within occupations that utilize verbal aptitudes. Sociologists as well as the general public have begun to ponder the source of these differences. This was the theme of a letter addressed to Dr. Joyce Brothers.

I work in a neighborhood nursery school. As a feminist I am shocked to find that little girls are a lot more passive at a very early age. The boys are a lot more trouble, and they are apt to strike out and hit someone. Since we get them at age three, I wonder if this is something in the training before they get to us, or is it related to their sex?

Dr. Brother's answer was,

Boys at all school ages, even nursery school, are more quarrelsome and aggressive than girls. Is this aggression inborn or due to conditioning? This question is still a matter of debate and one can find evidence to support either side.

Anthropologist Dr. Ashley Montegue points out that the male tends to be more aggressive because he has a lower threshold for frustration than the female. Society accepts more aggression from males than from females all through life. Females have demonstrated their desire to be more aggressive through participation in sports. In many instances they have competed favorably with men in such areas as tennis, track and field events, and basketball. Society still associates certain sports with the masculine gender as emphasized in the following questions addressed to Dr. Brothers.

We have four children, but only one son, and my husband has tried to dominate his life. I think my husband wanted a pal, a son who loved sports as much as he did and who would share his enthusiasm for hunting and fishing. Our son tried to be what he knew his father wanted, but now at age 11 he has given up on trying to please his dad. He confessed to me that he hates hunting and is bored with competitive sports. He likes music and wants to be in the school band. I told my husband this, and now he is afraid our son is going to be a homosexual. What can I do to get these two back together and on a good father-son relationship?

Dr. Brother's reply was,

Try to convince your husband that a love for sports and hunting has nothing to do with sexual preference. Virility is not related to combative sports. A love of music or poetry does not mean someone is less virile. Encourage your husband to let your son develop his own potential and to accept him as an individual rather than as an extension of himself. The parent who tries to relive his own life through his child, smothers his offspring, and the child usually resents this interference. Fathers who push sports on their children usually drive them away from games they might otherwise enjoy.

As this letter implies there are parents who want to live vicariously through their children.

These letters to Dr. Brothers also illustrate that society is trying to assimilate the changes taking place in the area of gender identity. The letter from the little boy's mother indicated a willingness to permit the child freedom to deviate from what the "macho" father desired.

ARE WOMEN WEARING THE PANTS TODAY?

If families have been affected by these changes, industry and our economy have been affected even more. Women have joined the ranks of corporate leaders demonstrating their desire to be liberated from societal norms. This trend began in the 1970's and has expanded to an all time high.

The trend of placing women at the top has been more pronounced in government related positions and in larger corporations. Women have proclaimed to the world that they want to be treated equally in the world of sports, work and education. The more avid supporters of the Equal Rights Amendment are demanding equal rights and equal pay. It seems that many women have been successful in crashing through the social mores and social expectations. Many are "wearing the pants" both literally and figuratively.

If the Simon theory is correct in the assertion that masculine and feminine behavioral patterns are greatly overlapping, we will certainly see liberation expand to include men. The predetermined life script does not seem to appeal to all men anymore.

Some have declared to the world, "Sugar and spice and everything nice, that's what little boys are made of too." The crossdresser is showing the desire to be "sugar and spice" through feminine clothing and through the expression of feminine feelings.

The one remaining hurdle relates to the fact that society is not yet fully ready to accept this male personification of sweetness. This type of resistance was spelled out in an article by Dr. Brothers. One reader wrote,

> I am seriously involved with a young man who is interested in becoming a professional ballet dancer. He has been in several shows already, and his coach feels he has a chance for a brilliant future if he continues to study. Whenever he comes to my home I am embarrassed because my father and brother are not able to hide their irritation and disgust. They think he is a sissy, and I am wasting my time on him. They are dead wrong, but I can't possibly convince them. I can't help getting angry, because I don't want to hurt my friend. I'm also angry because I get some of what he is getting when people refer to me as a tomboy, just because I don't waste my time sitting around doing nothing when I could be active. What can I do?

Dr. Brother's reply was,

> I suppose you might take them to a ballet performance and ask if they think there is anything weak or effeminate about some of those powerful leaps. Studies show that men who place so much emphasis on their definition of virility have hidden fears of homosexuality. They are also

unable to express tenderness and genuine warmth. This limits their ability to be good husbands, good lovers and good fathers.

This reply points out that some members of society, because of their own fears and insecurities, may resist the changing role of the American male. The crossdresser, however, appears to be secure in his own male identity and is able to move away from "macho" behavior and away from expected social norms.

Mass media, especially in the form of advertisements, has caused men to break away from the typical "macho" image. Clifford Pugh, a HOUSTON POST feature writer, has cited examples of how advertisers are showing a new side to the American male. Pugh describes a commercial in which a healthy young baby sits in his mother's arms. This is nothing new for an ad. What is new is that the father is standing behind wrapping his arms around his wife and Brand X of baby powder. The message given here is that it's OK for a father to be loving, kind and helpful. It is also OK for a father to share in the care and nurturing of children. In another commercial a father is cooking bacon while the children watch. The message given by this ad is that cooking is an OK activity for a man. The fact is most chefs are men.

A CHANGED MASCULINE LIFE SCRIPT

It is difficult to know if the current trends in advertising have caused changes in attitudes, or if mass media has picked up on a changed masculine life script. This is a, "What comes first; chicken or egg?" phenomenon. If advertisers are in fact following a national trend, this tells us "macho" is being liberated. I believe that this decade will place an emphasis on humanness. The dichotomy separating genders will be replaced with a continuum of human characteristics. People will be able to choose where they will stand and what percentage of masculine and feminine gender he or she will assume. We will see the liberation of the total person. Differences will be minimized while commonalities will be accepted. This change could benefit the crossdresser since crossdressing is becoming more socially acceptable. Today's male is already different from the typical male of a decade ago. He purchases hair dryers, fancy underwear and cologne for himself.

The whole area of men's and women's roles is changing, says Joe Kilgore, Executive Creative Director of Ogilvy and Mathes, an advertising firm in Houston, Texas. Kilgore sees the change as sharing, not role reversal. The Director of Research for the Cunningham & Welsh advertising agency is prepared to document this sharing of roles. According to the agency, of 1,000 husbands surveyed, 80% now take out the garbage, 47% vacuum, 41% wash dishes and 49% cook complete meals. It seems clear that the traditional roles are changing for both men and women. Perhaps gender is not set in concrete after all. The stagnation of gender role expectations has given way to an evolution that is exciting and complex. We have not come to this point without resistance. Breaking away from social mores and sexual stereotypes has stirred reactions of prejudice and ignorance. Fortunately, there are persons, both male and female, who are secure enough to move without fear toward the evolution of their total personalities.

Don Juan is quoted as saying, "Man likes to think of himself as bold and bad. The truth is that he is actually neither of these." The crossdresser has chosen to replace "bold and bad" with "soft and beautiful."

TRANSVESTISM - ONE STEP OUT OF MACHO

The stance assumed by women will surely make the situation easier for the crossdresser. To state this in the most simplistic terms, it seems only fair for him to be allowed to wear the dress if she is so insistent upon wearing the pants. It seems as if there could be a domino effect that will lead all the walls built around gender to come tumbling down,

> And all the king's horses and all the king's men
> Will not be able to put them together again!

Breaking down those gender walls will be beneficial for everyone, even the people who think this is not for them. There has been a disturbing trend among liberated women to adopt a double standard. They want their feminine prerogatives intact even as they butt heads in the boardroom. And many of these same women consider it an invasion of their space if their husband dons a dress. Previously men have been very much on the defensive about any manifestation of femininity. Yet femininity is present to some degree in all men. The men who become aware of this reality and learn to accept, without guilt, the feminine elements present in their personalities, are usually better integrated in their personalities and emotional status. They discover that there is a place for sugar, spice and everything nice, even in men.

It is important to point out that the woman who serves as a corporate head may still be a good wife and mother at home. Likewise the crossdresser does not sacrifice his masculinity by his enjoyment of feminine activities. He can still be a good father and husband. Wives and other family members who can understand this fact discover that the person involved is really a much broader, and more understanding human being, precisely because of his integration of masculine and feminine personality traits.

In many cases in which the wife and other family members object to crossdressing, social conditioning may be responsible. They object because they feel they are "suppose" to object. Not that many years ago women did not wear slacks, become police officers or company executives. Ten years from now men may be permitted to express femininity openly, without fear of ridicule, or feelings of guilt. It is all relative to time and social recognition of the fact that men have feminine qualities and women have masculine qualities. While women may openly express masculinity, men are condemned if they show any feminine qualities or traits. Hopefully the next decade will see men existing on a love principle and forsaking some of the more traditional ideas.

CHAPTER THREE

A NEW
MALE IMAGE

While femininity was once synonymous with mystery it is men who are the mystery today. What is the **new male image**? Only time will answer this question. We are not certain how men will respond to the changes within society that affect gender identity. The exaggerated awareness and assertion of masculinity in its tough, bold state seems to be giving way to a more emotional, feeling, masculine image.

During the past decade women have become much more open. Many women have flooded the media with information about their "real identity." They talk openly about frustrations, fantasies and hang-ups.

This openness combined with the changing role expectations for women have left men pondering what their roles should be. Most men do not like the label "brute" that many assertive women have placed upon them. Men seem to be resisting the idea that they have no feelings and no emotions. There has been an increased awareness of what could be called the **new male image**. At this time the image is blurred, but it appears that the veneer of fearlessness and dominance has been diluted. When the new image is fully within focus we may see an American male who is more domestic, sensitive and caring. This pattern is already evident in the typical crossdresser.

RESISTANCE TO THE TRADITIONAL MALE ROLE

Many men have become confused by the feminist movement. The confusion is not totally directed at the concepts of a new, more assertive role for women. In most cases it also relates to the fact that many people have stereotyped men as void of feeling. The more liberated male is tired of this rubber stamp. He is boldly resisting the idea that men have no feelings and emotions. Many men also feel repulsed when women assume the previously all male characteristics. In an interview on the CBS Morning News, Richard Nixon said, "Women lose something by becoming as crude, as ruthless, and as vulgar as some men are." In a discussion about the news media, Nixon said, "We have to realize that men can be tough, but women reporters think they have to be tougher; they've got to prove something." In the interview Mr. Nixon predicted, "There will be a woman vice-president within this century, and they are going to do that not because they are like men, but because they are like women." To date we have had one woman, Geraldine Ferraro, who unsuccessfully made her bid for the office of Vice-President of the United States.

While the typical man feels annoyed by some of the aggressive moves made by women many men are ready to pass some of the leadership roles over to the fair sex. They are prompted by statistics showing mortality rates to be eight years earlier for men. Meanwhile the women, caught up in the glamour of invading the man's world, appear eager to climb the corporate ladder. Current statistics are showing that stress related illnesses, such as heart disease and high blood pressure, seem to have a higher occurrence among executives regardless of sex. Entering the "man's world" may reduce the life expectancy of many women.

Organizations to promote women's rights are now two decades old. With this organized effort to change the feminine role there has also been the need for male counter organizations such as the Texas Fathers for Equal Rights. The purpose of this organization is to counsel men in matters such as property settlements, child custody and divorce. To date this organization has supported four bills introduced in the Texas Legislature designed to correct what its members consider unjust laws favoring women. These men feel abused emotionally, sexually and financially. They are now loudly asking for an equitable position within today's society. Many feel that this is not an easy time to be a man.

EVOLUTION OF THE TRUE GENDER IDENTITY

Crossdressers are probably the most classic example of one group of men that has resisted the traditional expectations thrust upon them by society. They are permitting the evolution of their true gender identity, which is a blend of masculine and feminine traits. They are looking inward for a softness that can be used to temper a hardened world. Some theorists believe that many crossdressers are looking back in time to their early childhood when there was shelter, warmth and love in the arms of a woman — usually their mothers. No one knows for sure about this theory or any of the other etiological theories which attempt to explain crossdressing. What we do know, without doubt, is that most crossdressers find release from their masculine gender roles through the experience of dressing as a woman and expressing those parts of themselves which society permits only to women.

I believe crossdressers are a generation ahead of society in the evolution of the true gender identity. As I have visited with them, I perceive individuals who have found inner security and self-awareness. The crossdresser has been able to crash through societal mores and traditions. He has been successful in expressing his total personality. He has walked over the parameters previously drawn that separated masculinity from femininity. His outward demonstration of this is feminine clothing. Crossdressers have solved the mystery of the **New Male Image**.

It is highly probable that many men have a desire within themselves to express femininity but fail to come to grips with this need because of fears and insecurity related to their own masculinity. Most crossdressers have had to deal with this reality. Once they are in touch with their total self many say, "It feels good to express love and compassion." They feel that touching all aspects of femininity is synonymous with touching all aspects of humanness. It is even possible that some of them understand the feminine side of their personality better than the masculine side. Crossdressers believe that love of the feminine can be aroused at any age and in numerous ways. They feel this love of the feminine feels very natural. It is a thread linking most crossdressers to the totality of life.

I know this is true in the case of my husband. He has assumed the feminine name, Melanie, to honor the feminine personality that has always been a vital part of his total self. Soon after my introduction to Melanie she told me her life story. This helped me understand more clearly. I believe this story supports my theory that crossdressers are in tune with the true gender identity.

Melanie is a classic example of a person who believes in and exemplifies the new male image. Her story tells of the struggles, challenges, and victories of a man who came to understand that life can have a greater dimension when the new image becomes clear.

MELANIE'S STORY

When I was a young child I had beautiful, long curly hair. People frequently commented about my appearance. They would tell my parents that I was too pretty to be a boy. I am not certain if these comments affected how I presently feel about femininity. Perhaps at this early age there was the discovery of how it feels to be beautiful. Even now when I get dressed in a beautiful dress there is the memory of what it was like in my early childhood years when people commented on how pretty I looked. From time to time people will still tell me that I have beautiful eyes and hair. This pleases me because beauty is a goal I have for Melanie's appearance.

Another strong memory from childhood relates to my mother. I saw her as having all the better qualities I wanted to emulate. She was kind, loving and generous. I wanted to be like her. Many people seem to think that crossdressers have some woman in their life worthy of emulation. This is probably true, and for me this person was my mother and more recently my wife. When I dress as Melanie I want people to see me like them. This is difficult to accomplish since I spend so much time in the business world where I am forced to be the aggressive, unemotional boss. It is difficult for love, patience and generosity to fit into this role expectation. When the work day is over and I have the opportunity, I rush home and shed my masculine clothing for Melanie's beautiful clothing. When I am into my feminine self I feel good and content. It is almost as if I can shed the pressures as my clothing changes.

To me being a crossdresser means that I can experience all the finer qualities of life that may not fit my life as a man. I enjoy being a loving person; I enjoy being like my mother and my wife. For me to give up crossdressing is out of the question. Why should I? I believe that my reasons for crossdressing are positive rather than negative. 1) I love beauty and enjoy being beautiful; 2) I want to become more like my mother and wife; and 3) I feel a release from occupational pressures when dressed as a woman.

I believe my experiences as a crossdresser support the theory that men become crossdressers in an effort to feel gentleness, kindness and love in a more dramatic way. When I change my clothing from clothing worn by a man to clothing worn by a woman I have a crutch that helps me show those qualities of femininity. It is like having the stage set for me so that the feminine role can be experienced. While these feelings can not be totally explained it seems that an early illness may have contributed. At age four, I became ill with polio. There was a great amount of love and attention showered upon me by my parents and everyone around. At the age of eight years a series of major surgeries needed to repair the damage caused by polio was begun. These surgeries necessitated long periods of time spent in hospitals. During these hospitalizations I experienced the pain of watching deaths all around me on the ward designated for polio victims. Frequently I became the counselor for the other children on the ward who were facing certain death. Several children died before my eyes as I talked with them. These harsh early experiences planted the seeds for caring, feeling and softness — those qualities usually associated with femininity. As I grew older I incorporated those feminine qualities into my personality. Through my crossdressing I am able to visibly express my feminine side.

As a young child most of my time was spent with my mother and grandmother because my father worked long hours. My father had difficulty expressing love and affection for me. We frequently had difficulty in communicating with each other. With my mother there was a higher demonstration of affection and love for me. The same type warmth was felt from my maternal grandparents, both of whom possessed what could be described as tender, warm, loving, feminine qualities. I have the idea that part of my need for crossdressing relates in someway to this very large need to be touched and held. I know other crossdressers who had parents who believed that boys should be touched and loved.

As a child I was seldom in association with what could be called "macho" behavior, and I did not care to relate to the typical stereotypes of maleness. While my father did not openly show love he did not demonstrate negative masculine behaviors either. When I look back to those days it seems that he was very busy providing for our material comforts. Since the time of his retirement he has been much more open with emotional expression. Today I see him as an excellent role model.

At age twelve I was a member of my church school choir. We performed in long, silk robes. I can remember the growing excitement of wearing the silk robe. There was a sensuality of feeling the silk softness next to my body. Since some of our choir concerts were held in the summer it was very hot in the church. I frequently wore my robe with no other clothing except underwear. I had the sensation of wearing a fine, silk dress. This was the starting point of my crossdressing. Soon I began to wear the robe at home on occasions when I was alone. I also began to develop a curiosity about my mother's clothing. Many times I went into her closet to feel the material of her beautiful dresses. There was also an interest in looking at women's clothing in catalogs.

One day I saw a pile of nylons in my parent's bedroom. I felt a strong attraction to the hose. I became transfixed with the idea of trying on a pair. I took a pair from the pile and slid them gently onto my legs, feeling intense pleasure as I walked around in them. I experienced an erection and felt intense sexual pleasure. This emotional experience caused me to feel guilty. I wrestled with a lot of social conditioning that condemns this act completely. Two days later when I was home alone I felt a compulsive desire to try the hose on again. This time I spent more time admiring my legs, running my hands over the smooth, silky surface and enjoying the intense pleasure this activity brought me. Despite the guilt feelings I began to wear the hose at every opportunity.

Soon I also became interested in the variety of high heeled shoes my mother owned, and I discovered that the shoes fit me perfectly. From that time when I wore the hose I also wore a pair of the high heeled shoes. I enjoyed walking around the room admiring myself in the mirror and feeling very feminine. Since both of my parents frequently were at work for one or more hours after I came home from school I had time to enjoy my new found enjoyment. The sexual feeling I experienced when I wore the clothing caused my to feel guilty and ask myself if I was a homosexual or if I was sinning. I began to think of myself as perverted. This led to an effort to compensate for what seemed to be a distorted gender identity. I began to work hard to develop a macho image around my friends and schoolmates. I joined the school basketball team. I wanted to be seen as being rough and tough. I wanted to prove to myself and others that I was 100% male. In retrospect it seems that most of all I was trying to prove something to myself.

In the meantime the compulsion to try on my mother's clothing became stronger in spite of my macho behavior in the neighborhood and at school. I discovered several of my mother's dresses that appealed to me. Since she was much larger than me, her dresses hung loosely on my body and failed to give me much satisfaction. I was thin at the time and could wear a size eight dress. Lying in bed at night I would fantasize about having a beautiful, feminine wardrobe complete with makeup and accessories.

At age thirteen I began to be attracted to girls. This attraction was based largely upon how they looked in their clothing. I envied them and wished that I could have their wardrobes. I dreamed of being dressed as a girl when I was with my girlfriend.

By age sixteen I had reached a point of believing that the only way to demonstrate my masculinity and keep my sanity was to give up my crossdressing. This decision was prompted by an experience I had one day when I was crossdressing at home. My mother arrived home from work sooner than I expected. Hearing her car in the driveway I quickly removed her clothing. She perceived my nervousness and questioned me. Her suspicions were aroused because she found me totally undressed in her bedroom. I finally showed her a pair of her nylons and told her that I had tried them on. She was upset but would not discuss the matter with me. She never mentioned this to me again and to this day, even though she knows I am a crossdresser, will not accept or attempt to understand my crossdressing.

My resolution to end my crossdressing was short lived. A few months later I began dating a girl who was very pretty. I always admired the way she dressed. I wanted to wear her beautiful clothes. One night we were alone at her home because her parents were out of town for the weekend. We were sitting on the couch in the living room, and I told her how beautiful she looked in her dress. She must have read my mind because she asked if I would enjoy being dressed as a girl. I told her that I would look silly in her clothes. She suggested that we cancel our plans to go out and have a dress up party instead. She was from a wealthy family and had fabulous clothes. She selected a complete outfit for me including dress, slip, bra, garter belt, nylons, high heels and jewelry. She also selected one of her mother's wigs. After I was fully dressed she helped me with my makeup. She led me to the mirror and told me she thought I made a beautiful girl. I could not believe the image I saw in the mirror. My dream had come true.

This experience was repeated several times when her parents were out of town. At times we left her house with both of us dressed.

We went to shopping centers and attended movies as if we were two high school girls out on the town. I looked so convincing that no one suspected that I was a man dressed as a woman. I began to feel like a complete woman.

In time this relationship ended but not because of my cross-dressing. I did not crossdress again until my senior year of college but continued to fantasize about being with my girlfriend dressed as a girl. I continued to date a variety of girls through high school and college but was primarily attracted to their clothing and femininity.

I married my first wife shortly after graduation from college. I thought about telling her my secret but was afraid that she would think I was perverted. Rather than tell her of my desire to crossdress I went the opposite direction and decided to permanently end my desire to crossdress. To me this was a demonstration of my masculinity. My attraction to my first wife also related to her feminine wardrobe more than to her personality.

The opportunity to tell my wife of my need to crossdress occurred three years after we were married. I was employed by a large hospital and spent much of my time walking the grounds of the institution. Because of polio my legs continually hurt. One of the staff physicians suggested that I wear support hose. I mentioned this to my wife and she agreed it was a good idea. I purchased the hose and a garter belt. I began wearing the hose continually. At night I enjoyed sitting on the couch watching television while wearing my hose and a long silk robe. I told my wife that I enjoyed wearing the hose. She asked if I wanted to be a woman. I told her that I did not but was attracted to feminine clothing.

She could not understand what I was telling her and concluded that either I wanted to be a woman or I was homosexual. After several days she told me that as long as I did not want to be a woman and was not homosexual she could accept my need to crossdress. Almost immediately I bought a pair of sheer nylons and wore them with a very feminine garter belt and panties. It was apparent that my wife would not accept my wearing the sheer nylons and panties but was willing to go along with this if it made me happy.

Over the coming months I added other items of feminine apparel. My clothing included a dress, slip, bra, high heels and wig. Because of my wife's insistence that I not dress at home I dressed when I traveled on my job. Since I was a psychotherapist by training I began to do a tremendous amount of reading of everything written on the subject of crossdressing, transsexuality and homosexuality. I quickly became convinced that there were thousands, if not millions, of men who shared this need. I knew I was not homosexual. My interests were in women and not men. While I did enjoy making love pretending I was a woman there was no desire to give up my male sexuality. I did not consider wanting to become a woman. There were times when I wished I could spend several days as a woman, but I had no desire to be locked into the role. I always wanted to return to masculinity.

All of this made me feel completely guilty. I would then go through the purging ritual of tearing up the clothes or burning them swearing that never again would I dress as a woman. This promise to myself was usually broken quickly. The interest would be rekindled when our new Sears Catalogue would be delivered. I would immediately turn to the woman's clothing section and again the desire to dress would become strong. No matter what my conscience dictated in the form of guilt I knew that the desire to crossdress had to be satisfied. This cycle was repeated at least five times over a twenty year period. It was expensive and stupid!

My wife's lukewarm attitude toward my crossdressing soon changed to total nonacceptance. I began to look for excuses to go out of town so that I could crossdress. Sitting alone in my hotel room I would wear the new clothes I had purchased, but there was always the reoccurring feeling of apprehension followed by guilt. These feelings tarnished what would have been supreme pleasure. I went through times of questioning my own self-worth and identity. At times I wanted to stifle the need to crossdress and be just a "normal" man. In 1968 I discovered a journal for the heterosexual crossdresser called TRANSVESTIA. I began to request information about organization memberships. I purchased the book written by Virginia "Charles" Prince, THE TV AND HIS WIFE, and attempted to share the contents with my wife. She told me that she would not have that "garbage" in her house and threw the book into the fireplace.

My marriage could not be complete because I could not be myself — a combination of masculinity and femininity. Without this I could not love my wife completely. After we had our second child there was very little crossdressing except the few times I had to travel out of town. Later we returned to Texas and moved into a beautiful new home where I began to dress frequently after the children were in bed. My wife would permit me to wear only certain items of clothing usually limited to lingerie. At times, however, she seemed to enjoy my crossdressing and asked that I dress in lingerie when we made love. This step toward acceptance ended abruptly and dramatically when she found some letters I had received through my private post office box from other cross-dressers. One letter, which I had not opened and read, apparently was from a crossdresser who was bisexual. His letter implied that he wanted to meet me with the possible result of becoming intimate together. I was not interested, but my wife didn't know this. At the time she found the letters I was leaving the next day on a business trip to California. She told me that if I went on the trip she and our daughters would be gone when I returned. She feared that I was making the trip to California to meet another crossdresser for sexual purposes. She was convinced that crossdressers were just another group of homosexuals who enjoyed making love to other men when dressed as women. This may happen with some men who crossdress but usually occurs because they do not find an understanding and accepting woman. I went to California as planned. My wife took our daughters and went to her parent's home.

I found out that while we were separated my wife shared the letter with her parents. She also told our daughters about their father's crossdressing. Her parents told her I was obviously homo-sexual, or I would give up this form of behavior. After a six month separation we began seeing a counselor. The counselor explained to my wife that he knew I was not homosexual and that my crossdressing was unusual but not abnormal. He encouraged her to accept my need to crossdress. She believed the counselor, asked that we reunite, and promised to do everything she could to accept my crossdressing and my feminine self. For the next three years she permitted me to dress when we were alone or when I was out of town.

Other problems emerged in the marriage, and she moved in with her parents. Her father told me that unless I promised to give up my crossdressing forever that he would see to it that his daughter obtained a divorce. I told him that my wife would have to seek a divorce. I would not give up a part of myself. Within six months the divorce was final.

Soon I met a young woman who herself had a great need for positive reinforcement. We both had a terrific hunger for warm strokes and appreciation. I knew soon that she was not secure enough in her own identity to accept Melanie. On one occasion I described a friend who is a crossdresser. Her reaction was something just short of disgust. From her comments, I knew that acceptance of my crossdressing was not possible. I thought that I would never find a woman who could understand and accept Melanie. Within three months of the divorce I met my wife, Peggy. I knew instinctively that I had found someone who would accept and love Melanie. We were married just eight months after we first met. A month after we married I explained my need to crossdress and asked for her understanding and acceptance. My dream had become reality. Peggy, as you can tell from reading this book, is Melanie's number one supporter. I am now complete as a person. I can now express my feminine side whenever I desire, and at the same time my masculine side is stable and secure. I have also become more successful in my career because I feel fulfilled. The new male image for me is being a total person.

Peggy has expressed our feelings in the following poem:

MELANIE'S NEW IMAGE

We have closed the door to the past.
We have obscured the glare that prevented
A beautiful view of the here and now.
Joy has come at last.

The detours of yesterday
Were nothing more than deterrents.
Our lives are filled with contentment
As we permit our love to guide the way.

A new image of my being has emerged,
The old image is washed away.
Feeling new, complete, and whole
I know the old image has been purged.

Fantasy has become reality
As the last frustrations melted away,
A confidence now abides in our hearts,
And our lives are blessed with serenity.

Hold my hand, oh my darling!
Together we will share the rest of our lives,
We are finally complete,
And with this completion our hearts will sing.

CHAPTER FOUR

WHAT IS FEMININITY?

There is a common thread running through the stories of all crossdressers — they love femininity. This was demonstrated by Melanie's story as she expressed a love for beauty, a love of tranquility felt when away from the task oriented world of career, the love of a mother's compassion, and a love for feminine qualities as expressed by her wife. Melanie also told of her love for women's clothing. She prefers the softness of women's apparel to the rough textures used for men's clothing in the business world.

Since love of femininity is characteristic of all crossdressers it seems appropriate to devote an entire chapter of this book to explaining the meaning of femininity. One thing is clear at this point—crossdressing is love-motivated. Crossdressing could be called more of an expression of admiration than an idiosyncracy. The unfortunate thing is that the women who are so greatly admired are sometimes the first to "cast the stones."

The greatest problem in organizing the material for this chapter was obtaining a good definition of the word "femininity." Giving an accurate definition of femininity is difficult for at least four reasons:

1. Femininity is different things to different people.

2. Dramatic sociological changes have altered the preconceived ideas about gender.

3. Not only is society changing but so are individuals. Therefore views about certain sociological phenomena such as femininity are in a state of evolution.

4. For the most part society tends to think of femininity and masculinity as opposites. In reality gender should be considered a continuum of human traits. Some of these traits are more prevalent in males; others are more prevalent in females. No one knows where to draw the line between masculinity and femininity.

Since masculinity and femininity are sociological in nature they can not and should not be considered static. They are constantly changing as society itself changes. We can think of the masculine traits clustering on one end of a continuum. Activity, intelligence, courage, and industry are positive masculine traits. Other masculine traits such as aggressiveness, insensitivity and coarseness are negative.

At the other end of the continuum are feminine traits that are positive including kindness, sensitivity, tenderness, warmth and love. Other feminine traits such as weakness, passivity, emotionalism and timidity are negative.

No rational man would want to be 100% masculine with both the positive and negative traits of masculinity previously described. The "macho" male is frequently so eager to avoid the stigma of feminine traits that he may conduct himself in an unnecessarily aggressive manner. In terms of the continuum, he locks himself into a constellation of traits that will leave no doubt that he is "all man."

Similarly women who abhor the feminine traits of weakness and passivity may also resist some of the more desirable positive feminine traits. The feminists have frequently assumed negative masculine traits since they also abhor the status assigned them within society. Men become crossdressers for many reasons, but the common thread that runs through the story of each crossdresser I have met is that somehow those magnetic, wonderful, desirable feminine qualities have had a strong positive influence on their lives. For this reason they are characterized by a love of femininity in its positive sense. Frequently because of career demands crossdressers must occupy a portion of their lives in the negative masculine self-imprisonment. This provides the crossdresser with a greater appreciation of the more positive feminine qualities. Perhaps the best definition of a crossdresser relates to his mobility on the gender continuum. He changes position more frequently and dramatically than most persons, though all persons change positions from time to time. He is not limited to antiquated gender roles. His emotional range is greater. He moves from the personification of masculinity to the personification of femininity, but his goal should be to stay on the positive side of the continuum as much as possible.

THE GENDER CONTINUUM

intelligent	insecure
courageous	gruff
Industrious	brutal
compassionate	tough
caring	coarse

MASCULINE

Positive_____Negative

FEMININE

kind	insecure
sensitive	bossy
tender	rude
warm	self-centered
loving	whiny

Crossdressers, as a group, recognize the qualities within their psychological composition and desire an expression of these traits through crossdressing. This may be the main difference between the crossdresser and men considered to be "normal." There are times, however, when the crossdresser may want the world to see him as normal. At this time he will put up a macho front and will outwardly move away from the image of femininity. Within his heart there is still the realization that feminine qualities exist and he struggles to identify them.

In the spring of 1977, GLAMOUR MAGAZINE attempted to define femininity. The authors of the article had conducted a survey. According to Ruth Whitney, Editor of the publication and coordinator of the research, the responses came back on post cards, in handwritten notes, and on crisply typed letters. Some women wrote their responses in the form of poetry on notebook paper. Others used office letterheads or flowered-scented note pads. The definitions of femininity supplied by the readers were as varied as their written form. When the magazine had sifted through all the survey responses and organized the contents, they found that the responses could be grouped into five basic categories.

FEMININITY IS LOVE, CARING AND NURTURING

Love, caring and nurturing are equated with femininity because these characteristics are thought to be synonymous with virtue. Traditionally women have been considered virtuous. Since early times the woman's life script called for her to be gentle, wise and understanding. She was expected to react to environmental stimuli with compassion and empathy. This image of femininity was characterized by submission and the desire to be passive to the point of self-sacrificing or martyrdom. A woman cared for the needs of her family, loved her children, and tucked them under the covers at night. Society has fostered this definition as ideal and perpetuated it by teaching young girls the traits needed to assume the feminine role in the future. I believe the crossdresser tends to relate to this definition of femininity very well. He finds himself in a society that fosters a stereotyped male image. His life script demands that he be dominant, assertive and aggressive. When this happens many perceive this "pseudo macho" image to be only a veneer. Beneath the detached, impersonal, forceful, competitive exterior exists a warm and loving side. One crossdresser remarked to me, "Deep within me there is a tender side crying to get out. I'd like to kiss away the tears of the child who has fallen and skinned a knee. I would enjoy tucking the children in at night. I want to be able to feel and experience softness and tenderness." Could it be that the crossdresser is one who chooses to express rather than repress femininity?

FEMININITY IS BEING YOURSELF

Femininity can best be expressed by the woman who knows who she is and what life priorities fulfill her. She has established goals and is clear about where she is going with each goal. To her femininity might just as well be expressed in blue jeans, but if the occasion demands, she is equally comfortable in Brussels Lace. Her feminine side will usually be dependent upon the need of the moment, upon the occasion, or upon her present mood. Most of all she has the flexibility to change as circumstances change.

The crossdresser also has a deep desire "to be myself." He recognizes his own feminine traits and is confident that this "second self" is a reality. He actively resists society's demands about his gender identity. Unfortunately, when he does not meet the expectations set by family, friends and society there can be conflict. He decides either to deny himself self-expression in crossdressing or confine it to secrecy. The woman who perceives some expression of masculinity as positive and fulfilling for her life has the blessing of society; but the crossdresser who expresses femininity risks rejection. Society has given women the right and opportunity to be assertive and bold, but the same society vigorously denies men the opportunity of expressing feminine qualities.

As a group crossdressers recognize that the expression of both masculine and feminine traits is good. An emotionally secure femmophile is able to say, "I am a unique individual and I can express femininity and still be OK." Reaching that point in the development of his self-awareness, he is able to move into what Glamour magazine calls, "the total and uncompromising state of me." This state goes beyond a mere appearance of femininity into the state of possessing, feeling and expressing femininity. The crossdresser who describes femininity as "being myself" is one who loves the sensuality of expressing his second self. He feels that life has afforded him an opportunity of exploring all facets of his identity and perfecting his feminine attributes. When he dresses as a woman he may say, "Femininity is the aspect of my private life that makes me feel good about myself and the fact that I am, for a part of my life, a beautiful, feminine creation." The crossdresser who embraces this definition has gone a step beyond the traditional image of womanhood. He has also gone beyond the simple wearing of clothes that are usually only worn by women.

FEMININITY IS LACE, LINGERIE, BUBBLE BATH AND ROSES

Lace, lingerie, bubble bath and roses are the outward indicators of an inward feeling. One respondent to the Glamour survey said, "Femininity is a state of mind. It is a feeling I get every once in a while that makes me linger in a bubble bath or lazily paint my nails, enjoy a beautiful love story, or sew a long lace dress with ruffles."

These aspects of femininity relate to doing something about what is inside. Femininity is equated with looking sexy so that you can be seductive and please your lover. "To me," wrote one respondent, "femininity is a woman's personal ability to bring out the best in her man, to make him feel confident, important and loved, to be able to sense and fulfill his needs."

These are tangible manifestations of intangible feelings. When the crossdresser begins to permit the feminine side of his personality to emerge, he will get in touch with his feminine feelings. He may enjoy the aroma of Chanel No. 5, admire the beauty of his own eyes that are accented with a blush of color, and begin to project these feelings to others. When the crossdresser begins to feel femininity he will find the true fulfillment that he has been searching for. He will permit feminine gestures, postures and habits to occupy the personality of the second self. He will feel some of the joys of womanhood.

FEMININITY IS JUST BEING A WOMAN!

About 80% of the Glamour magazine respondents said in essence that femininity is the ability to enjoy and take pride in being a woman, and the ability to convey those feelings to others. These women feel both psychologically and sociologically a creature of beauty. They harbor no desire to appear masculine or dominant. These women probably are not involved in the woman's liberation movement, since they do not wish to be liberated from their status.

The crossdresser also is seeking the right to feel both psychologically and sociologically a creature of beauty. He enjoys being a woman and knows that by experiencing femininity he is expressing the totality of his humanness. Many times the sociological manifestations of his feminine self must be dormant except within organizations for crossdressers or at home.

FEMININITY IS BECOMING A TOTAL PERSON

Many persons wish to express themselves fully, but it is the crossdresser who is in touch with both the masculine and feminine traits and attributes. They have done extensive soul-searching, and feel that the expression of both genders is desirable. By day they may command a corporation with hundreds of employees. By night they may see the positive feminine traits emerge. They are capable of being very feminine, perhaps even passive and dependent. During the day they may obtain pleasure from their accomplishments on the job. When they are away from the job and have the opportunity to crossdress, the pleasure comes from just being a woman. The two parts together make up the total person.

As I have visited with crossdressers I have found that there is a great variance in how far they will go in being a woman and expressing their femininity. Some have a simple fetish for one garment or one type of feminine apparel. Others wish to live out their lives full time as women. Men who want to go beyond feminine apparel into the more intense feminine traits and qualities will profit from looking again at these five descriptors of femininity — for within them rests a full interpretation of the word.

To feel more feminine the crossdresser should:

1. Permit himself to love, care and nurture in a feminine manner.

2. Move on ahead toward being himself.

3. Permit himself to enjoy feminine feelings. He could look for pleasure in the expression of these feelings through wearing lace, through soft lingerie, through bubble baths and roses.

4. Enjoy BEING a woman for at least part of his life.

5. Permit both masculinity and femininity to be expressed. By doing so he will be complete.

6. Move freely on the gender continuum, but remain in the positive constellation as much as possible.

CHAPTER FIVE

THE CROSSDRESSER AND HIS PARENTS

Parents, almost without exception, want the best for their children and have special concerns for their son. Even when the child is a young boy, mothers and fathers begin to project plans for the future. These plans usually include a college education, a successful career and the "happy-ever-after" marriage. It may be difficult for many parents to divorce their own identities from their children. Many parents have a difficult time when their child's interests, aptitudes, or abilities fail to match their own. There seems to be special concern when a son does not match his father's image of masculinity. The father's interpretation of gender is seldom broad enough to include crossdressing.

If the parents of a crossdresser would take the time to question their son, they would probably find that he looked for opportunities to express femininity. As a younger child, the son may have worn his mother's or sister's clothing whenever possible. When he grew up and left his parent's home he may have purchased his own feminine apparel. He might tell of feelings of guilt that prompted him to discard his feminine clothing. The son may have realized that to meet his parent's expectations of masculinity he could no longer continue crossdressing. Usually this "reformation" is short lived. The typical crossdresser finds that forsaking his desire to crossdress is very difficult.

It is possible that we have observed a father who turned red with rage when he found his son playing with dolls. According to psychologist, Henri Parens, the rage is sometimes fueled by a fear that the son has feminine behaviors. Perhaps their greatest fear is that the son may become homosexual. "All of this is nonsense," said Parens, who directs the early child development program at the Eastern Pennsylvania Psychiatric Institute in Philadelphia.

A little boy who plays with dolls is not doing anything feminine. More specifically he is doing something parental - identifying with the father. If we want him to grow into a father who is loving and considerate of children, it would be a disservice to discourage him from experiencing these kinds of feelings when he is small.

This illustration shows how parents tend to overreact when the behavior of their son deviates from the norm. With these pre-established patterns of behavior by parents, it is not difficult to understand the total chaos that may result when parents discover that their son is a crossdresser. Many parents do not have the insight into the physiological, psychological, or sociological rationale for crossdressing. They simply can not cope with this disclosure, at least not initially.

QUESTIONS ASKED BY PARENTS OF CROSSDRESSERS

The first question heard from the parents of a crossdresser is, "Where did we go wrong?" It will help parents to know that there is no proof that crossdressing is caused by parental mistakes. In conversations with parents, many also express the fear that their son has some psychological or emotional problem. This has not been proven either. If these are not the causes, parents want to know what does cause crossdressing. Medical research has indicated some correlation between the crossdresser's **genetic balances** and his need to crossdress. The **genetic push theory** is one possible explanation. According to this theory all embryos are the same until the sixth week of the prenatal state. At that time a genetic push occurs. A protein substance is released. This is the catalyst for the development of male traits. Some people believe that in the case of the crossdresser the "push" is inadequate. While crossdressers are born male sexually, much of their emotional state remains feminine in nature. Crossdressers say that they feel feminine and want to express feminine traits and attributes.

The third question frequently asked by the parents of a crossdresser is, "What is the cure?" The best way to answer this question is with another question, "Who has the right to judge what an individual wears to cover the human body?" The answer that ultimately will be given is SOCIETY! Our society dictates that the wearing of feminine clothing is not appropriate behavior for men. Perhaps we need to take a look at the social system that has caused our inhibitions. Should a man feel guilty or embarrassed if he has the desire to wear women's clothing? Could it be that society needs to be cured and not the crossdresser?

HOW CAN PARENTS HELP?

After evaluating their son's disclosure of his crossdressing, parents need to ask , "What can we do to help?" The best way to provide help for their son is through love, understanding and acceptance. Parents need to know that their son is attempting to express a side of his personality that is in contrast to the aggressive, dominant male traits. Their son is wanting to express the more passive, tender and loving qualities he has found in his own femininity. Some have suggested that crossdressers may be looking for a way to escape from some of society's expectations for men. If parents can show acceptance and verbalize a love that is big enough to encompass their son and his crossdressing, his conflict and feelings of guilt in not meeting their expectations will be reduced considerably. Parents must come to the point of saying to their son, "We will show our love for you by accepting you as you are!" In the book, SEX AND SOCIETY, (Pelican Books), Drs. Walker and Fletcher stated that transvestites are not sick, therefore no "cure" for them is needed. According to these authorities, "It would be better to treat the society which makes it so difficult for these unfortunate people." In a very broad sense the expression "unfortunate people" is not appropriate. Parents will be helping their son if they can come to think of him as "fortunate." He is fortunate because he is one of a group of men who has permitted the total personality full and unrestricted expression. He is fortunate because he has let the more positive personality traits emerge.

THE BEST "TREATMENT" FOR CROSSDRESSERS

In a study conducted by Johns Hopkins University, two researchers, Money and Russo, concluded that an environment that is nonjudgmental is probably the best "treatment" for the crossdresser. In their research Money and Russo studied 11 boys with prepubertal disorders of gender identity. The boys were studied through young adulthood. The patterns of femininity did not diminish, but self-esteem was greatly enhanced in situations where acceptance was evident.

The development of an environment of acceptance is not an easy task for parents, especially since they must work through a series of anxiety producing questions. However, it is possible for love to grow into the type of family commitment that will overcome negative feelings. My own mother and father-in-law have had difficulty accepting their son's crossdressing. They live their love in every aspect of their daily activities but somehow it is difficult for them to reach beyond confusion in regard to their son's crossdressing. They found out about his need to express femininity ten years ago. My stepdaughter, who knew of my husband's crossdressing, decided to tell them. We do not know her reasons for making the disclosure. We do know that this knowledge has caused my husband's parents to feel anxiety and tremendous pain. Realizing how they must feel I decided to write them a letter. The purpose of the letter was to ease the pain, tell them of my own awareness, and explain how I had personally come to grips with the situation.

Dear Mom and Dad,

I know that the discovery of Mel's crossdressing has
been very hard for you. My hope is that I can help you
during this time of adjustment. Having been through this
experience myself recently I will be able to reach out with
love and understanding.

It is very good that this news came to me from Mel
rather than someone else. This has helped. In a letter he
explained his need to express the feminine side of his
personality by wearing female clothing. When the letter
was complete he brought it to me in my office and left me
alone to absorb the contents. When I read the letter I felt all
kinds of tension. It was as if Mel was gambling our relationship for a wardrobe of feminine clothing. Since I already
had some knowledge about crossdressing I understood
what the letter described. I still felt fears. This began an
introspection that lasted through the next several months.

Our wedding vows were still in my mind. They ultimately gave me strength as I repeated the vows to myself
one more time. We had written these words as an expression of our love and commitment: "Because God has given
us life and the love we share this day, we commit our love
to each other. Together we will honor God as husband and
wife as long as we both shall live. Together we will venture
into life, clinging always to the faith. Together we give all
we possess spiritually, emotionally and physically. In love
and sacrifice we will share together the love of God. His
light will lead like a guiding star. Therefore we promise
this day to live with the happiness of each other as our
ultimate goal. We promise to share both joy and sadness,
sickness and health, poverty and riches as long as we both
shall live."

After reading the letter and remembering the words of
our wedding vows, I knew that for Mel's happiness to be
complete I must become committed to accepting him exactly as he is. Mel's confession to me was followed by a

series of problems with the children who knew of his crossdressing and refused to accept it. There were times when I felt the load was too heavy, but I found strength and a quiet peace. Knowing that I have given him understanding and acceptance has provided Mel an inner satisfaction and fulfillment he never previously experienced. I receive much joy from seeing him so happy and complete as a human being.

Science has stated that no man is 100% male in his hormonal constitution. The average man may be closer to a 60/40 ratio. The same proportion may hold true for women, but society has permitted women more liberties in clothing and personality expression. Some psychologists have stated that the crossdresser may be more secure than other men. Perhaps this stability is related to the fact that he is in touch with positive feminine characteristics such as compassion, love, affection and tenderness. Unfortunately little boys are frequently taught that they should suppress this portion of their personalities. Mel and other crossdressers are willing to permit an emergence of these traits, despite what society dictates.

At the same time, Mel is happy with his masculinity. He enjoys being admired by women and has absolutely no tendency to be homosexual. He is a much warmer person because of his ability to crash through social restrictions. In short, he is a fantastic husband and father. Mel knows that I have accepted him as he is. We have adjusted very well.

During the day Mel continues his life as a man. In this role he is "all man." At night he becomes Melanie — a beautiful woman. In fact when Mel is Melanie he looks very much like you, Mom. He finds complete relaxation and peace of mind in the role of his second self. We will talk some more soon. Do not feel in any way that you have failed as parents. You are blue ribbon parents and we love you both very much. Just remember that the qualities he manifests as a crossdresser are love, compassion and warmth. These are beautiful qualities. Remember that he learned his best qualities from your good examples. My prayers are with you.

Fondly,

Peggy

After my mother-in-law and father-in-law read the letter I think they tried to accept the contents. However, years of social conditioning have clouded their thinking on the subject. Frequently they say things to my husband like, "We surely hope you appreciate that wife of yours. Nobody else could understand or accept you the way she does." For the most part their behavior is characterized by avoidance.

Crossdressers frequently ask if they should tell their parents about their crossdressing. This is an individual decision, dependent upon the personality of the parents and the relationship between the crossdresser and his parents. Great care and love must be exercised if the parents are told. One thing is certain, the crossdresser should be the one who makes the disclosure.

RESEARCH ON CROSSDRESSING

Since the early 1980's a few researchers have addressed the subject of the crossdresser and his parents. In a doctoral dissertation completed in 1983, Dr. Jack H. Goldfarb hypothesized that an individual's gender identity is determined to a great extent by his or her parental identification patterns. Goldfarb's research indicated that crossdressers who manifest some disturbance in their gender identity may show a pattern of identifying with the parent of the opposite sex.

It is the father who is the paramount influence in the lives of crossdressers according to David W. Drueger of the Baylor College of Medicine. In an article published by the American Journal of Psychiatry, Drueger tells of a crossdresser who fathered three sons, all of whom engaged in crossdressing by their teenage years. The article stated that the father played an important role in gender choice and modeling.

Two Australian researchers, Buhrich and McConaghy, stated that many mothers of crossdressers had hoped for a girl prior to the birth of their sons. They also reported that many fathers of crossdressers lacked interest in their sons and were frequently absent from the home. Buhrich and McConaghy asserted that crossdressers tend to have a pathological relationship with their mothers. Yet Virginia Prince conducted a study involving 504 crossdressers. The study indicated that no more than 05% of the respondents reported that their mother wanted a girl when they were born, nor did the mothers treat them as if they had been born a girl. Moreover, absentee fathers were not common either. In defense of the Australian research, my husband's parents wanted a girl prior to his birth. He looked like a girl when he was young and was frequently told he was too pretty to be a boy.

According to researchers Rekers, Lovess, Bentler and Rosen, the only thing parents can do to prevent their son from becoming a crossdresser is to look for signs of an affinity for femininity and take action to submerge the feelings. There are several definite problems with this plan. The crossdressers I have talked with have said that even at an early age they knew they had to hide their desire to crossdress. Also efforts to suppress femininity may create severe emotional and physiological problems. A 17 year old crossdresser was taken to a psychologist by his parents to find a "cure" for his "abnormal" behavior. After several months this young crossdresser began to suppress his expressions of femininity. He wanted to please his parents and the psychologist. After several months the pressures began to affect his emotional state. One afternoon his parents found him dead in his bedroom. He had dressed in his mother's clothing and then shot himself in the temple.

There are parents who realize that their son has a "problem" with gender identity. No one is certain what has caused this "problem," and what the "cure" may be or even if the "problem" should be "cured." Frequently the primary problem is the attitude the crossdresser and his parents take toward the behavior. I have reached the following conclusions based upon my study of crossdressing:

1) Crossdressing is a sociological phenomenon and NOT a psychological or medical problem.

2) There is NO cure for this behavior apart from acceptance.

3) The parent's responsibility begins and ends with their own openness to their son's crossdressing.

4) Many authorities believe crossdressing has its origin in the prenatal state.

THE AGE OF HUMANNESS

We have seen a great expansion of the social and political roles for women. Before liberation can expand to include men we must divorce ourselves from the doctrines that assume the genders to be separate. It is time we thought more of humanness and less about gender roles. Once the rigid social norms have been broken, persons will be able to move their positions within the gender continuum. Differences will be restricted to physiological and anatomical factors only. We know that sex is dichotomous. Gender need not be.

One of the main problems we have had is we do not separate sex and gender. If we can realize that gender traits such as aggressiveness, decisiveness and fearlessness on the masculine side, and gentleness, tenderness, and sensitivity on the feminine side are not sexual indicators, then and only then will we be able to comprehend crossdressing.

CHAPTER SIX

THE CROSSDRESSER AND HIS WIFE

The husband and wife relationship is clearly the most intense of all human commitments. The deeper the love the greater the vulnerability to hurt. Understanding this basic concept helped me unscramble the emotions related to my husband's crossdressing. I felt severe frustration when he told me that he was a crossdresser. I was shocked and full of disbelief. There were times that I resorted to feelings of personal inadequacy or even guilt. It was threatening to know that my own femininity was not enough to hold my husband's attention, and he needed his own feminine expression. Other emotions included anger, uncertainty and rejection. At first I felt totally alone, and it seemed that no one else in the whole world could be experiencing such a problem.

It soon became apparent that my husband's crossdressing had a negative effect upon our lovemaking. There were times when my husband was self-centered. He didn't even notice that the lingerie he wore was a turn-off for me. His thoughts were more on his pretty clothes than upon my sexual needs. I wondered if God could help me understand what was happening in our marriage. The first time I kissed Melanie I felt guilty. It was like being a participant in a lesbian affair. If pushing a magic button could have made the situation go away, I would have pushed the button. I wondered if sex would ever be the same again, and if I could ever be the same. Crossdressing seemed morally wrong. I perceived the problem to be a power struggle. I wanted to order my own life and somehow crossdressing interfered. My life was being controlled by something I had not heard of a year before. The person that I married was being suppressed while a feminine side was emerging larger than life.

Fear and apprehension were real. Many questions flooded my mind. What if our family members find out? Is my husband gay? Will my husband want to have a sex change? What about my husband's job? What happens when the neighbors see my husband dressed? Will our friends still associate with us if they find out? Will we be rejected? Will we be ridiculed? I struggled to find answers.

It seemed that one surprise followed another. I found myself asking, "What will be the next shock?" When I grew to one level of acceptance my husband always wanted to add some new twist. Also crossdressing was becoming very expensive. We were the couple with three lovely wardrobes.

DEALING WITH THE PROBLEM

Despite these negative emotions there was the reality that crossdressing would not go away. It would always be a part of our lives. Therefore I knew it must be dealt with. There are two levels of acceptance, intellectual and emotional. Intellectual acceptance seemed easier. I knew it was wrong to judge my husband, and I also knew to accept my husband's femininity there must be an acceptance of myself as a woman. I started thinking of this problem as a growth experience. The fear seemed to be directly related to a lack of understanding. My desire to learn more was very real.

We started to talk more about my husband's crossdressing and his need to express femininity. Our communication involved listening to each other and discovering what our specific needs were. We also negotiated solutions. Our horizons began to expand to what made each of us happy. Looking back it seems that acceptance went through phases. Confusion came first. This was followed by resentment and fear. I then went through a time of "putting up with Melanie's odd behavior." This was the indulgence stage. At this point crossdressing seemed like a "whim." Once I realized that crossdressing was more than a passing fancy we were on the path toward adjustment and acceptance. I wanted to move to a full emotional acceptance. For me this meant that I must put aside some of my own self-pity and self-interest. Without my acceptance Melanie was incomplete as a man and incomplete as a woman. With my acceptance Melanie found the totality of humanness. It is like being born again. Thus the song, BORN AGAIN, became our favorite song, because it expresses the need for crossdressers, like Melanie, to be whole. Wholeness means full expression of masculinity and femininity.

BORN AGAIN

Come bring me your softness,
Comfort me through all this madness,
Woman, don't you know with you I'm born again?
Come give me your sweet lips,
Now there is with you no meekness,
Lying safe with you I'm born again.
I was half - not whole,
Content with none,
Reaching through this world in need of one.
Come show me your kindness,
In your arms I know I'll find this.
Woman, don't you know with you I'm born again,
Living safe with you I'm born again.

Even as we knew that an aspect of our relationship had been born again, there was the realization that another part had died. The traditional values set by society for marriage could never exist for us. While this may seem like a morbid description, the situation could best be described as like death. I cried, and then I cried some more, but in time there was the realization that everything would be fine. It was true that there was a great loss. The good news was that there was a new avenue for our happiness. I conducted the equivalent of a symbolic funeral.

Yesterday was buried. Now we will look toward the future to see what new and wonderful things are in store.

LETTERS TO PEGGY

While our story is a good example of the growth process that can occur, there are other stories that should be shared. I have included one letter from a crossdresser. He describes the agony of not being accepted. Joy and frustration can be felt in the letters written by several wives. Following each letter I have included my response to them as their counselor. My hope is that you will find help vicariously through these letters and my responses.

THE ANGUISH OF NOT BEING ACCEPTED

Dear Peggy,

For the first five years of marriage I felt that my wife was not secure enough to be told of my desire to crossdress. From reading and from discussions with other femmophiles, I came to the conclusion that a wife must be mature, open-minded and stable if she is to successfully cope with having a crossdressing husband. Nevertheless I finally broke the news to her through the purchase of a silk slip for myself. She asked if this meant that I had a desire to wear other articles of feminine apparel. I confessed that for years I had wanted to be totally dressed as a woman and on occasion had done so when alone. Her reaction could best be described as one of shock, and I knew at once that she could not accept this part of me. From time to time I wore the slip under my masculine clothing. At other times I wore only the slip around the house. Because of her discomfort with this I frequently had a feeling of utter frustration. I tried to reduce my need to crossdress by becoming involved in a lot of activities, but this didn't work. Also I tried to be macho like my wife wanted me to be, but this was like living a lie. A large portion of me was feminine and this could not be denied. To express love meant expressing strong feminine qualities, and my wife would not permit this. Soon I was given the label of homosexual. She could picture me in my slip making love to another man. This was not true. Never in the ten years of marriage did I have any desire to share sexual experiences with a man. My love was always for womanhood. In short I wanted to love a woman with a feminine kind of love. All of my best efforts to work things out failed. At the end of ten years my wife filed for divorce. I have no regrets about the divorce except that the children have suffered. She continues to tell them things about me that are not true. It hurts to know that they see me as some kind of pervert. Even the children are trying desperately to get me to suppress the desire to crossdress. While this may be possible for short periods of time I know that I could never give crossdressing up completely. It feels like I was born with this desire. Any efforts to suppress the desire have always resulted in physical illness, antagonism, and a feeling of being incomplete.

As I write to you, Peggy, I am still single. I have tried to find a relationship that could include crossdressing, but so far this has not happened. If you know of any women in the Houston area that are open-minded enough to accept a crossdresser please keep me in mind. Give my regards to the members of Tau Chi.

Sincerely,

Pat

My response:

Dear Pat,

Thank you for the long informative letter. I have thought a lot about your failed marriage. It is probably too late to help with that relationship, but perhaps I can help you see how future relationships can be improved.

The best way to inform a wife or girlfriend about crossdressing is to start with matters of the heart. Tell her how you feel. Praise her wonderful feminine qualities, and explain that you would like to demonstrate these same qualities in your own life. Most women have been taught that positive traits such as gentleness and caring are admirable in both men and women. If she can accept these qualities as a part of you she will come closer to accepting your desire to crossdress.

Unfortunately as you discovered in your first marriage some women are not taught this way. These women really need a macho male and will not be happy unless they are with one. They seem to seek men who are are aggressive and domineering. They suffer from verbal and often physical abuse from these so called wonderful, "macho" men they are attracted to. These men would not be caught dead in a dress, but neither would they permit themselves to express any feminine emotions. Women with a preference for macho tend to be manipulative and restrictive of crossdressing. It is a no win situation. As you found out, the desire to dress can be suppressed for a short time, but it can never be eliminated.

As you continue the search for the right wife look for a woman who admires the more gentle qualities. When you find her be sure that she knows how much you admire her as a woman. Good luck in your search for Miss Right.

Sincerely,

Peggy

COPING WITH JEALOUSY

Dear Peggy,

My husband has expressed the desire for two contrasting life roles. He told me that he wants a masculine and feminine identity. I am doing everything possible to help him. For example when he comes home from the office after a tiring day his feminine clothes are already laid out for him. We share ideas about clothing, makeup and hair styles. It has been fun watching him improve the feminine image. He has progressed from a clumsy amateur toward a high degree of expertise in his crossdressing.

In most ways I could be labeled an A wife according to the Virginia Prince rating scale, but I know in my heart that there's still room to improve my attitude. Since I fell in love with a man I want my husband to love me as a man loves a woman. He needs some kind of prop in order to be sexually aroused. By this I mean that he needs to be wearing some kind of feminine clothing when we make love. I am willing to compromise. It would be fine if we made love this way a part of the time, but I feel deprived knowing that the only way we can make love is as one woman to another. I am not a lesbian. I don't like being made to feel like one.

I have another problem that could be called jealousy. In his job he takes other women out to lunch, and will also meet women in bars to discuss business. That sounds rather harmless, doesn't it? I know that he is not interested in them sexually, but when I am present in these business meetings I see a lot of touching. Going out to dinner and going to clubs are the two things we do for entertainment. The thing that I have asked myself is this, "If these women get to go out to lunch with my husband, and if my only experience of love making is with my husband dressed as a woman, what do I really have?"

I have thought a lot about this. I think that my husband's female business associates see more of the masculine side of my husband than I do. No matter how this situation is analyzed this seems unfair. If going out to dinner is the thing we do together this should be reserved only for me. Also some of the love making should involve my husband acting like a man and loving me as a man to a woman. Please tell me if I am being unnecessarily jealous. I love my husband very much, but somehow I feel that my needs have fallen by the wayside. My husband married me, not these business associates. I feel that at least a part of his masculinity should be reserved for me.

Love,

Frances

My response:

Dear Frances,

It sounds like you and your husband need to reach a compromise. I believe that he should make love to you in a way that will make you feel that he is a man. This needs to be discussed. There will also be times when he will want to express the feminine side of his personality during love making.

It is true that you married a man and not a woman. He has an XY chromosome pattern and male hormonal characteristics. You must realize that he loves you as a man to a woman even when he wears a see through gown, but his erogenous zones and sexual feelings may be more feminine than masculine. Remember also that most cross-dressers are very faithful. While he may admire some of his business associates the chance of him being unfaithful are less because he is a femmophile. It sounds like you are doing a great deal to meet his needs. If you continue to do this he will be faithful for life. Communicate what your own needs are. In time he will understand that you have given up much of what is considered "normal" sexual experience and he will make a stronger effort to meet your needs. Your needs must not be sacrificed.

Learn to think of love as the regard for the total person. It is impossible to sort out the various aspects of personality and say, "I'll love this part of you but not that part."

Femininity is a very real part of your husband. Hopefully your husband knows how fortunate he is to have such liberty to express himself in your home. Good luck in your efforts to reach some compromises. Keep the lines of communication open. Listen as well as talk, and try to feel the needs of each other. I feel confident that you will work everything out.

Love,

Peggy

LEARNING TO ACCEPT THE CROSSDRESSER

Dear Peggy,

I am married to a crossdresser and there is nothing I like about it. Since the first time I saw him in feminine attire I felt that an injustice has been hurled at me. I'll never forget the first time I saw him dressed as a woman. I had been working late, and found him sitting on the couch fully dressed in a red dress and a wig when I came home.

Upon entering the den of our home I could see an obese woman sitting on the couch. She was wearing red nail polish, and a lot of makeup. She had four inch black high heeled shoes, and strong perfume appropriate only for a French whore. Beneath a mask of makeup and jewelry I could see my husband. My heart pounded wildly, and I stood with my mouth open just short of speechless. What I felt was a combination of repulsion, disgust and anxiety. I turned my head, but the image was still there. I did not want to talk. I did not want to see. Walking away in frustration I soon found things to do at the other end of the house. As they say, "Out of sight, out of mind." After numerous delays I found my way back to the den. Much to my dismay "IT" had not gone away, "IT" had not faded into the woodwork, and "IT" had definitely not changed clothes. He/she was sitting patiently waiting for what I considered a masquerade party. It wasn't even Halloween! He/she reached out for me and planted a kiss on my lips. The clod! Laughing childishly I replied, "Now I know what you guys dislike about lipstick. Ugh! that taste awful! You don't know the first thing about makeup. I hope you know that you are wearing too much eye shadow. Your lipstick is too dark, the wig is a mess, the jewelry is very overstated." By the last comment my husband had lost all interest in sex. I had no interest from the moment that I first walked in the door.

One week later my husband asked if we could dress up together. I reluctantly agreed. We pulled out garter belts, dresses, hose and jewelry. On this occasion I saw humor in the whole thing. Can you imagine watching a 180 pound man pulling on a girdle? It was even funnier watching him struggle to fasten the garter belt behind the muscular, hairy legs. He then asked me to fasten the bra which he subsequently filled with foam rubber. Once all the padding was stuffed into the bra he walked to the mirror, turned to a 45 degree angle to admire his newly acquired curves.

Watching the makeup process reminded me of the time Dottie, our daughter, discovered makeup. My husband had the same perplexed expression as he smeared a glob of makeup all over his face. The end product was about the same as Dottie's also. The edges of the lips were smeared and the shape was somewhat distorted. The mascara looked more like spider webs than anything else. I began to understand why men plead so earnestly for women to go lighter on makeup. I remembered even my own husband saying, "Let your natural beauty show through!"

At this point I wished that he would take his own advice. I took another look at his face. It was so handsome. He has beautiful brown eyes, long, thick lashes, and a fabulous complexion. All of this was hidden beneath the makeup. My heart felt heavy as I longed to have my husband back. I longed to feel my husband's presence. The world stood still while I remembered falling in love with him. He had a smooth, masculine image and a charm that was charismatic. I can remember other people gathering around him almost as if he was a human magnet. I admired his career success. He seemed to be the perfect blend of charm, intelligence and task-orientation. It was comforting to know that he could provide for all my needs.

As I pulled myself back to reality I could see my charming, virile, handsome husband standing before me dressed as a woman. I walked outside, took a deep breath, and tried to sort out all that was happening in our marriage. Realizing that my husband would probably attempt to make love to me later while dressed as a woman reminded me of the Isle of Lesbos. On this island there was extensive sexual activities among women. The word "lesbian" was derived from these actions. The whole idea was repulsive. I did not want to go back into the house but soon found courage to do so. Meanwhile the makeup ordeal had been completed and my husband was lying on the bed. "Come here and lie beside me," he purred. I paused for a moment and looked at him. All of this seemed so alien. My husband had been replaced by an overweight female who looked like she was dressed for a burlesque show. I moved toward the bed, but there was a wall separating my emotions of that moment and the feelings that had always been reserved for my husband.

I felt like a male impersonator while my husband had painted on an image of femininity that was distasteful. Everything seemed unnatural. Sensing how I felt my husband turned away from me and seemed to move into a state of despondency. He soon lost all desire for me and wept quietly upon his pillow. He knew that because of my feelings about lesbianism and crossdressing in general that I could never help him fulfil his greatest need. As I write this letter today it's difficult to know where we are going from here. All my ideals about marriage have been eroded. At the same time it is perfectly clear that my husband's needs have not been met either. It seems like there is another person within him crying out to be freed. I do not know this other person, and I miss my husband when this other person invades our home. I am afraid that I am not secure enough within my own identity to help him find a solution.

I am asking for help. Saving our marriage is very important for both of us, but we really don't know how to go about it. We would appreciate any ideas you might have in helping us to find a solution.

Love,

Lee Ann

My response:

Dear Lee Ann,

Your husband is moving too fast for you. Encourage him to give you time to adjust. It is clear that you need to sort everything out. It is not realistic to expect you to make love to a stranger, and that is exactly what the feminine side of your husband is. I would like to see you get to know the feminine qualities that he possesses. You will probably find this part more lovable than the masculine side. This is the case with my own husband. Mel has a temper. Melanie is the one easiest to love. He is in love with femininity and tries to emulate all the better feminine qualities. Loving this part of him will probably add dimension to your marriage.

It will be fun teaching him what you know about makeup and clothing. Your husband is on the same level as Dottie. It reminds me of the Rockwell picture of the twelve year old girl looking in the mirror at her newly acquired womanly body. The teddy bear, now abandoned, lies crumpled on the floor. Both your husband and Dottie are experiencing some aspects of womanhood for the first time. I'll bet that you didn't treat Dottie's tentative, hesitant efforts with icy, sardonic responses. Try to gently make suggestions to them about makeup and clothing. You will be amazed how fast they can improve with your gentle help.

Your husband will never be a physiological female. This is not what he wants for himself. Femininity, on the other hand, is a psychological and sociological matter. Your husband wants to share this with you. He wants to cross over the line and view the world from your vantage point. Invite him into your world. He is not interested in you only as a sex object. He is interested in all aspects of your life. In time when some of your pain has gone away, crossdressing may even bring happiness to your life together. He probably places you in higher esteem than you place yourself. Give him a chance to demonstrate that he is in tune with your needs and desires. He knows what you want better than most men, because femininity is so real to him. You have a husband who understands your need for pretty things. What also needs to occur here is an exchange of concerns for each other. Reach out and help your husband understand how to reach out to you.

Perhaps it would help if you knew that your husband's need is not unique. Crossdressers are found among all segments of the population, but they are most frequently found in the group of men who are highly educated and successful. A survey of crossdressers indicated that over 70% are married and have children. You are not alone.

The key to acceptance is love. Your letter was full of love. You probably want his happiness as much as anything else in the world. Know that you alone hold the key to his total happiness. Once you have permitted him full expression of this feminine side his love for you will grow even greater. Both of you will need to demonstrate this love by compromise. By mutual agreement set up a time when he can crossdress. When he buys himself something new and pretty you should also get something. As was mentioned earlier encourage your husband to give you enough time to assimilate all of this. Such an experience is traumatic for a wife, but I believe your love is strong enough to see you through. You are not being asked by your husband to be a lesbian. He realizes that you are a biological woman. It is your kind of femininity that your husband loves. Please keep in touch with me. I will anxiously await the news of your progress.

With love,

Peggy

IS CROSSDRESSING MORALLY WRONG?

Dear Peggy,

I am a Christian and crossdressing seems morally wrong to me. Our minister mentioned a scripture in the Old Testament that says men should not wear women's clothing. Are you familiar with this passage? What do you think about this? Have you ever felt guilty because of your husband's crossdressing? Do you think that a man is sinning if he wears women's clothing? My husband is very religious but feels that his desire for crossdressing is acceptable to God. He serves as a lay minister in our church. His desire to wear female clothing is the only real problem we have in our marriage, and I really need some answers.

Robert is one of the most loving, sensitive men I have ever met.

I attended a seminar that you led recently and felt that you could help me with this problem. I'll be looking forward to your answer.

With love,
Rachel

My response:

Dear Rachel,

It is difficult for me to say what is right or wrong for your own life. I do know that your question is a good one, and this matter needs to be addressed. There was a time when I felt that cross dressing could be morally wrong, but the more I study the issue the more I can see that for me there is no real problem.

The scripture passage that your minister mentioned is Deuteronomy 22:5. It says, "A woman shall not wear anything that pertains to a man, nor shall a man put on a woman's garment; for whoever does these things is an abomination to the Lord your God."

When I read this passage of scripture my first reaction had to do with my own actions. Just this morning I put on my husband's sweat suit and went out for a three mile walk. I really enjoy wearing his shirts when I want something loose and comfortable.

The more I thought about it the more I realized that in one regard I was as much of a crossdresser as my husband. The whole idea of me wearing slacks seemed questionable, but it occurred to me that this scripture was taken out of context and to understand the real meaning a person would need to look at the whole passage. At this time in Bible history women were not permitted certain religious rights. For one thing they were not allowed into holy places. In order to gain admission some women would disguise themselves as men.

Such scriptures are a part of Old Testament law. According to Christian belief, Christ came into the world to replace the old law. This replacement was good. Can you imagine what would happen if we stoned adulteresses today? If we consider crossdressing wrong, we would need to look at some other aspects of Jewish law. Are you willing to give up eating pork? This is not kosher. The law also stated that a man could not touch a woman during her menstrual period, because she was unclean. Women were excluded from the main house during that week. Would you enjoy sleeping in the garage one week out of every month? Under the law my iron skillet is too heavy to be lifted on the sabbath. I would hate to break the news to my husband that there will be no more bacon and eggs on Sunday! All of this sounds a bit extreme, but it does illustrate the point that these laws are no longer relevant in a modern society.

What is relevant is following Christ's example for right and wrong. He taught that we should love others as ourselves. He also said that we should do unto others as we would have them do unto us. Since Christ came to fulfil the law, faith is the essence of eternity. Christ taught that all men must come to him exactly as they are. I believe this includes crossdressers. I know that some may disagree with me, but I believe that crossdressers were born not made. If that is true we would be very wrong to not accept them. I do not believe God would like for us to use Christianity as an excuse to not accept our husbands exactly as they are. God's way is a way of love. I do not believe that love and acceptance of our husbands' need to crossdress is a contradiction to the Bible or the teachings of God.

Sincerely,

Peggy

OPEN LETTER TO A CROSSDRESSER'S WIFE

Dear Friend,

You have received the news that your husband is a crossdresser. The good news is that he trusted you enough to share a very personal aspect of his life. Millions of women have not been told. Either their husbands are afraid to tell them, or they do not want to share all of their life with their wife. You are fortunate that you have a relationship that is open. This puts you ahead of the pack.

The bad news is that this is not an easy thing for a wife to handle. You have experienced hurt, anger and disappointment to say nothing of confusion related to how best to handle this bombshell. Should you tolerate this, accept the crossdressing, or pack your things and get out of town fast before your mother finds out? Before you make a decision permit me to help you evaluate the options.

OPTION ONE:

END THE MARRIAGE

You could walk out the door, obtain a divorce, and leave him alone to enjoy his own femininity. This may seem like the easiest solution, but is this the solution you are seeking? Remember all the reasons that you married your husband. In all probability those reasons are still present. His better qualities have been distorted by the crossdressing. If you walk away you will not be able to forget the man you love.

Let me tell you emphatically that the grass is not greener on the other side of the fence. It is a man's world out there. If you are trained in a profession you will still have numerous adjustments. Life is not easy for a woman alone. You will find a world of men saturated in male ego who will not enjoy your success if you find it.

Jealous women in the work place may also cause you some problems. If you don't make it professionally you will struggle to pay the bills. There is one other little point of trivia. Who will fix the things that always seem to be broken around the house?

Having faced the world alone you may see the cruel realities of life and say, "Hey, I was married to a crossdresser and upon close examination of this man's world I think I can understand why he became a crossdresser." Ask yourself these questions: Could it be that my husband has grown weary within a male dominated society? Has he found release from these pressures through crossdressing? Allow me to tell you about one wife that decided upon divorce as the best option. She was not a professional, but moved back home with her parents and enrolled in college to obtain a degree in education. Life at home with her mother and father was not like she remembered. Time had conditioned her way of life and she no longer fit in as she once did. There were disagreements greater than any she had experienced with her husband. She realized very quickly that life without her former husband was more difficult than she expected. There were other men in her life, but even that was less than fulfilling. Most of them were eager for a "romp in the hay" but less than eager to make any kind of lasting commitment. They did not measure up to her former husband in any way. The bottom line was that she still loved her crossdressing husband. She actively tried for a reconciliation, but the husband had fallen in love with a young woman who had no problem with his crossdressing. There was no way he would give up a good relationship for one that had been less than rewarding.

Emotional problems soon surfaced. She was depressed and lost excessive weight. Soon there were physiological problems including asthma. Although she had graduated from college and had obtained a job as a teacher, she was financially destitute because of medical expenses. Conditions went from bad to tragic. Last autumn when the leaves began to gently fall, at 47 years of age she died during an asthma attack. She died with a broken heart.

As a counselor I worked with her former husband. I encouraged him to look toward the future. This he has done, and he is now very quick to help wives who can not accept their husband's crossdressing. He tells them this story. He is now married to a wife who accepts and loves him as he is. We all realize that this is an extreme situation, but it does help to prove that learning to cope is a better solution than escape.

OPTION TWO:
LEARN TO TOLERATE CROSSDRESSING

Let us now look at a second option. You may decide to stay in the marriage and tolerate the situation. With your tolerance your husband will find some release through crossdressing. He will experience the tangible side of femmophilia, the clothing. The problem is that he will not be able to experience the intangible aspects including true feminine feelings. If you stop at the tolerance only level he will be inhibited. He may feel guilty and embarrassed. There will be only shallow joy, because you do not really accept him totally. This he will know without being told. The complete union of a man to his wife will not be achieved, because the vows are built upon mutual sharing of the total life. He will feel less than complete, less than loved, and less than accepted.

OPTION THREE:
YOU CAN ACCEPT HIM JUST THE WAY HE IS

What is involved in acceptance? Acceptance involves a renewal of the original wedding vows. It involves realizing that marriage is a partnership. This is a mutual giving and sharing of the total self. The intent to alter the personality of another person is futile, and when we come to the point of acceptance there is no longer the desire to change the other person.

Acceptance involves communication. You openly talk about what your needs are and listen willingly to your husband's expression of his needs. When the needs are in conflict there is a willingness to compromise. With the compromise comes a feeling of satisfaction and approval. The wives I have talked with who call themselves, "accepting," believe that they have found a greater fulfillment because they are married to crossdressers. They express pleasure in sharing the whole life and discuss the new dimensions that are added as fringe benefits.

Reaching a level of acceptance is a challenge. As with most challenges you will be a better person once the challenge is overcome. There will be a time when positives outweigh the negatives. When this happens the road toward acceptance is within view. This is a goal worthy of your best efforts. With my best wishes for your journey toward acceptance.

Love,

Peggy

CHAPTER SEVEN

IMPROVING THE MARRIAGE

We live in an age in which divorce is almost as commonplace as marriage. From my observation it seems that the marriages of many crossdressers may be at greater risk than others. I believe it is about time someone asked, "Why?" Could it be that crossdressers have been so preoccupied with their own needs that they have not stopped to think about the needs of their wives? Could it also be that the wives of crossdressers are so locked up into what society perceives to be normal that they can not hear their husband's cries for help? This chapter may be used as a salve to heal existing wounds, or it may be used as preventative medicine. As the wife of a crossdresser I have come to the realization that the relationship my husband and I share has required a great amount of giving from both of us. While this chapter is written primarily for the wife of the crossdresser and the crossdresser himself, it may also have application for the woman who is dating a crossdresser.

Some wives of crossdressers I have talked with seem so hurt and confused they really can't verbalize what their specific needs are. Therefore I have prepared a global statement of what I consider the most fundamental needs of the woman who is married to or dating a crossdresser. These statements are generalizations and may not fit each individual situation. They should be a beginning point for each couple's communication.

BE HONEST ABOUT CROSSDRESSING

Something is missing in marriage when couples are not honest with each other. I would even say that honesty is one of the basic elements of commitment. Most wives want an open, honest relationship with their husband, but they may not be emotionally prepared to hear that they are married to a crossdresser. How does he tell his wife this? How can he be totally honest if he knows that the truth could end his marriage?

Honesty, even as related to crossdressing, is best, but the crossdresser must take the time to understand himself before he expects his wife to understand. In cases in which there have been problems, the crossdresser may not know how to communicate, and the wife may not know how to receive the communication. Since crossdressing is sometimes controversial, communication should be a special concern. Can the crossdresser express his true feelings if he is uncertain about his own identity? Self-awareness and self-honesty must come before the wife is told. Coming to grips with WHO he is and WHAT he is will require a large amount of self-analysis and effort on the part of the crossdresser.

Frequently the crossdresser will feel discouraged since there are only a few vague theories about the external forces that contribute to his internal identity. There are even fewer theories about the prenatal conditions that dictated his life as a crossdresser. He can face who he is in total honesty, and make great strides in self-understanding, if he will spend some time in reading, in study, in self-analysis and interaction with other crossdressers. When the crossdresser has developed self-awareness and an understanding of his inner identity the relationship with his wife can be faced with total honesty.

If there is love, acceptance, and understanding from both husband and wife, the couple will then be able to communicate and share their thoughts, feelings, desires, and emotions. The crossdresser is not being honest when he does not share these. Commitment to honesty in communicating emotions and feelings is a prerequisite to a stable marital relationship for a crossdresser or any man.

The crossdresser is in a most precarious position when he decides to communicate honestly about his crossdressing. He is gambling on the possibility of losing the relationship if his wife or significant other does not accept his crossdressing. There is a gauge that could help the crossdresser determine whether the relationship is solid enough for total honesty. This gauge is love. If the love is strong enough to include the recognition of individual needs, desires, limitations and individuality, then the love is strong enough to include the acceptance of crossdressing. Many accepting wives have said, "Of course I will take him as he is. I would never give up this wonderful person because he is a crossdresser. The price is too great!" Unfortunately not all wives feel this way at first. Some never do, because the love is not great enough.

BE PATIENT

Usually after the wife finds out her husband is a crossdresser she immediately experiences confusion, anxiety and hurt. She may want more than anything for her husband to hold her hand and guide her to understanding. Often the nonaccepting wife has been confronted by a defensive, insensitive and insecure husband. Acceptance and understanding of the husband's crossdressing will not happen overnight, and it is possible the process could take years. In the meantime the wife may experience symptoms of anxiety which can emerge in other problematic forms including nervousness, jealousy or irritability. The husband should not expect everything to be peaches and cream. He must not push her, but gently love her. In time many wives will realize that the assets of the relationship outweigh the liabilities.

Some readers may consider this wishful advice, since numerous women are not capable of acceptance. The totally nonaccepting wife may feel defensive, insecure or uninformed. The crossdresser must be sensitive to these feelings. If this does not work and the non-accepting wife feels there is no hope of resolution, they may be faced with a decision about the future of the relationship. They may have to consult with a professional to help sort out the confusion before the final decision is made to end the marriage.

HELP AROUND THE HOUSE

The wife may be more likely to accept her husband's need to crossdress if he is helpful around the house. It is such a contradiction when the crossdresser wants to enjoy the glamorous side of femininity and then neglects the menial side — such as washing dishes, making the bed, cleaning the bathtub ring, picking up the clothes on the floor, changing the baby's diapers, etc. Frequently I have heard this paraphrased comment from wives of crossdressers, "He says he wants to be feminine and beautiful, so he primps in front of the mirror while I clean the house. He steps out of the bedroom vanity looking like Miss America and I look like a woman appearing in an Ajax commercial."

If the crossdresser wants understanding and acceptance from his wife, he should help her finish all those menial tasks around the house. They could do the work together, then shower or bathe and get beautiful together. The wife will love it. The house will look nice, and the couple will be dynamite! After everything is beautiful they could get out the best wine and put on soft music. Soon the wife will feel that it is her special brand of femininity that has made her husband happy. He should thank his wife for showing him the steps to becoming beautiful. Neither person should mention the hard work that preceded the steps to beauty. This comes with the territory known as femininity.

BE BEST FRIENDS WITH YOUR WIFE

Most women want their husband to be their best friend. This can be a beautiful experience for both of you. Capture this as one potential strong point in your relationship and develop it to the fullest. I consider my husband my dearest friend. In many ways my relationship with my husband is similar to the relationship I experienced with my sister who is 22 months older. When we shared a room at home and later in college we talked about clothing, makeup, jewelry and those dear intimate thoughts that only girls share with each other. The friendship shared by a crossdresser and his wife can be similar to the friendship between two sisters.

Crossdressers are very unique men with special, feminine needs. Because of the nature of this relationship an accepting wife can be part of the evolution of the total personality. The wife can be a partner — a closest friend. This can be one of the most blessed aspects of an intimate relationship between two people who feel a deep love for each other. The word "together" has a special meaning for two lovers who are also friends. The crossdresser and his wife will soon discover that this type of relationship increases the joys of life and divides the sorrows.

Wives or significant others may want to share all of life, including both successes and failures. There is little danger of the crossdresser losing his own personal identity through sharing. Each person has his/her own personal identity, and yet as a couple there is a part of the life that includes both husband and wife. It is like two circles that overlap:

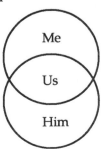

Some wives will feel honored when they are a confidant. It is a joy watching my husband grow both as a man and as a woman and knowing that he is confidentially sharing his life with me.

DON'T FORGET THE HUSBAND AND WIFE RELATIONSHIP

Many wives of crossdressers have a fear of losing the normal husband-wife relationship and most HAVE lost it to a greater or lesser degree depending upon the unique situation of each marriage. I have heard of numerous wives who fear losing their "man" completely through his possible future choice of sexual reassignment surgery. Others fear something less complex like not having her "man" in masculine form all the time. One wife confided in me recently, "I have never seen D'Wayne dressed as a woman. I'm not sure that I'm strong enough yet. It will be like losing him as a man when he's transformed into a woman."

Her husband should not rush the issue. Perhaps the wife should see a picture of her husband crossdressed first and get accustomed to the idea gradually. It might be too much of a shock to see her husband totally dressed in women's clothing. It sometimes helps if the crossdresser starts with only one item of clothing such as panties, a gown or hose. The amount of dressing should not exceed her readiness. Hopefully the wife will open her mind and try to be ready for the changes that are imminent.

The crossdresser should never shrug his shoulders and say, "Our relationship is not normal, therefore I do not need to participate in all the activities that characterize other normal marriages." This attitude is fatal, believe me. The crossdresser must find out what makes his wife happy. With acceptance follows a demonstration of masculinity from the husband. This is a small compromise. He should do the typical masculine gestures such as opening doors, helping with her chair, taking her dancing, and even letting her admire his masculine physique. The wife may soon realize she has the best of both sides - masculinity and femininity. The crossdresser needs to make his wife feel that she is his special woman. She is his image of femininity. He must take time to write her a love note, pick a wild flower and hand it to her with a kiss on the cheek. The age of chivalry is not dead, and the crossdresser's wife does not want it dead in the relationship. If the crossdresser withholds his masculinity, his wife will certainly resent his expression of femininity. I guarantee it!

One crossdresser friend of mine made an issue of these things. He did not want to be the typical male, and yet on one occasion the wife noticed that he carefully opened car doors if a second woman was in their company. To the wife this seemed like a double standard in which the "macho" image and behavior was reserved for the other woman but was not offered to the wife. Wives usually want this kind of special attention and will feel threatened if another woman receives the masculine gestures when she has not received them. It is only fair! The wife who helps her husband fulfill his feminine needs must also have HER feminine needs fulfilled also. The need to feel ALL WOMAN is not reserved just for the crossdresser.

One wife of a crossdresser describes how her husband wants to be dressed as a woman each time they make love. This bothers her because she feels like a lesbian when they make love. She would like to share some intimate times with her husband when he is not dressed as a woman. In this way she could feel that their sexual activity is closer to normal. She does not enjoy making love to her husband when he is enfemme, and she desires a heterosexual and not a lesbian relationship. This is a problem for many couples. It must be addressed, and the couple must reach some compromise. Unfortunately many crossdressers get selfish to the point of not reaching out to their wives' needs.

Many times in the past my husband resisted expressing his masculinity because he had negative feelings about his male image. I believe this feeling was the result of an illness that occurred during his childhood. I would see pleasure on his face when I would help him step from his masculinity, drop the veil and become feminine. During recent years the dormant side of his personality has been revitalized. He is now in touch with his femininity. The irony of the situation is that through this revitalization of femininity he has also become better adjusted as a man.

My husband wants to emulate a woman—me. I do not think of myself as a self-sacrificing martyr, but sometimes I engage in self-pity. Usually the thought of my husband, and the realization of his complete masculine/feminine self, will lift me from this destructive habit. I enjoy the feminine qualities my husband demonstrates in our relationship including his tenderness, sensitivity and love of everything feminine. I also enjoy his masculine qualities which focus on meeting my needs as a woman.

The crossdresser may express extreme disappointment, because his wife does not recognize or attempt to meet his feminine needs, while at the same time he may not recognize or attempt to meet his wife's feminine needs. The crossdresser needs to ask his wife what her needs are. It could be as simple as buying her a pair of new high heels or dress when the crossdresser shops for himself.

HELP THE WIFE ACCEPT CROSSDRESSING

I have included a list of suggestions for crossdressers to consider. These could improve the relationship with their wife or significant other and lead to acceptance of their crossdressing:

Strive to become best friends.

At least once each week go out together alone with your wife or significant other (s/o).

Ask your wife or s/o to help you grow both as a man and as a woman.

Demonstrate your masculine qualities.

Demonstrate your feminine qualities.

Be patient and wait for her to grow toward understanding and acceptance.

Make her feel like she is the most important person in your life.

Permit your love to grow and express it.

Let her help you with your problems and needs.

Never praise other women more than you praise your wife or s/o.

Never walk away when she is crying.

Never speak to her above a normal conversational tone.

Never physically abuse her — use your strength for love.

Do not criticize unjustly the things about her personality that may be difficult for her to change.

Do not reveal her faults to other people.

Do not destroy her pride and self-esteem.

Never forget that she wants to be treated as a lady.

Demonstrate kindness by speaking kindly, giving her flowers, etc.

Do not hold back your negative thoughts. Tell her what bothers you, but do so in a loving way.

Do not forget your commitment to faithfulness.

WHAT HAPPENS IF SHE DOESN'T ACCEPT?

The wife or significant other needs to understand and accept the reality that if she resists her husband's desire to crossdress he may experience insurmountable pain. The desire to crossdress will not go away. There is no cure! Frequently wives have told me that if their husbands really loved them they would give up this ridiculous "hobby." Many crossdressers have attempted to give up their crossdressing in an effort to make peace in their families but without success.

The goal of love is to share, to understand, to respect and to give mutually to each other. The crossdresser is not able to have a complete love for those who do not accept him, because there is no sharing, no respect and no understanding.

In a harmonious family life there can not be any areas of antagonism, hatred, or irritation that are not dealt with. In time these negative feelings will erode even the most positive aspects of the relationship. It is very common for one person to not accept or understand all aspects of their partner's personality. A relationship can survive these differences if the lines of communication are open.

WHAT IS THE ULTIMATE GOAL?

The wife and family of the crossdresser have to keep the lines of communication open with the goal of gaining understanding, and possible acceptance of his need to crossdress. It does not matter if he told his wife before or after marriage. He opened his heart and shared his ultimate secret out of love and trust. Now the wife must open her heart to him. Most of the crossdressers I have known have wanted to share themselves totally with their family members.

Many of the crossdresser's positive qualities are directly related to being a crossdresser. He has recognized those qualities such as tenderness, kindness or compassion as being beautiful. If the wife could push a button and erase her husband's crossdressing, she would also erase these positive qualities. Does the wife want this? Think about it. The wife needs to open her heart to mutual happiness. It is possible. She has to forget her role as the "traditional" wife long enough to fulfill her husband's needs. Her needs will also be fulfilled.

The personality of the crossdresser can never permanently change. Acceptance is the only answer. Such acceptance does not mean that the wife has to totally approve immediately. It means that she will perceive a situation that is irreversible and desire to seek the best from the situation. When she does this her tolerance will grow. The love the wife feels for her husband usually relates to the kind of person he is and not the clothing he wears. The clothing does not change him. Is her husband able to love and accept her when she is dressed in one of his shirts? What is the difference? When the wife breaks through this barrier and understands that her husband is not two persons she will reach the point of completion in her love for him. His crossdressing can serve as a sacred bond that unites both husband and wife. Once the crossdresser feels acceptance the wife will experience an outpouring of love greater than she has ever encountered. I have come to believe that the highest level of acceptance comes when the wife sees her husband as one person regardless of what he is wearing.

Research and medical studies have indicated that most crossdressers are above average in intelligence. Most are also married to women with above average intelligence. Intelligent and well-educated women are usually more flexible and open-minded. They are more willing to accept things that can not be fully explained or understood. Being married to a crossdresser can provide the wife with satisfying experiences. The wife may experience great enjoyment as she shops for beautiful clothes with her husband. Shopping trips to fashion stores will take on a dimension she had never previously experienced. She will begin to take pride in her husband's second self. I feel satisfaction when Melanie receives compliments on her clothing or makeup. After all Melanie is my masterpiece. I contributed greatly to her ability to look very attractive as a woman.

Some wives would enjoy participating in their husband's crossdressing if they understood the difference between crossdressing and homosexuality. They feel that these crossdressing activities are "kinky". What these wives should realize is that the crossdresser has a love for womanhood and not a love of manhood and men. They are the objects of their husband's affection. Most homosexuals do not have a desire to dress in woman's clothing. Homosexuals who crossdress usually do so to attract other men. A Kinsey report indicates that the incidence of homosexuality among crossdressers is lower than among the total male population. This is because crossdressers, as a group, are more loyal to their wives or significant others, and the crossdresser wears feminine attire as a means of expressing his inner feeling of femininity. The homosexual "drag queen" wears feminine attire to attract men for sexual purposes. For some homosexuals wearing feminine attire, and looking very flamboyant, may be their way of showing their contempt for women. The crossdresser places women and femininity on a pedestal. He loves femininity and everything femininity represents.

Women who have overcome these fears and have grown to the point of total acceptance are usually very satisfied with their marriage. They feel loved, admired and cherished. They all say that becoming totally accepting was not instant nor was it easy. To reach this level took compromise, tears and effort. But when asked if it is worth it, they answer in a strong, affirmative, "Yes, I am among the most fortunate!"

At some point these wives emerged from a grieving process not too different from the loss of a loved one. In many respects they have lost something they loved - an image of what they thought a husband should be. They have lost what traditional ideals dictate that marriage is. At some point a "funeral" was conducted in their hearts. Ideals were buried. But even as Easter symbolizes the resurrection of Christ, a new image of marriage was born. Once this grieving stage has passed wives of crossdressers are ready to open their hearts to one of life's greatest adventures! They are married to a crossdresser, and life is great. It may be different, but it is wonderful. This is the ultimate goal!

CHAPTER EIGHT

THE CROSSDRESSER AND HIS CHILDREN

Crossdressers who are married and have children are faced with even more complex problems than other crossdressers. There are many questions to be answered and issues to be resolved. Should we tell the children or not? If we do tell them when do we tell them and how do we go about it? What if they find out on their own? There are no universal answers to these questions. Each family must answer them within the limits of their own situation. The most important thing to remember is that the crossdresser does NOT have the right to make the decision without his wife's agreement and participation, nor does the wife have that right.

Young children are probably the most accepting, trusting, loving persons in the world. It would seem, therefore, that a plan involving total honesty with young children would be best. But is it? Many wives I have met flatly refuse to include the children. If the wife has this attitude, and the crossdresser tells the children without his wife's agreement, there may be alienation and hostility. This could lead to an eventual divorce. I believe that young children are basically very accepting and understanding of their parent's behavior and activities. They do not yet have the prejudices of most adults. In most cases these children could accept their father's crossdressing. The most dramatic reaction would probably be laughter and a comment like, "You look funny, Daddy." This would be their way of saying, in effect, that you do not look like other dads.

Most children are totally honest. They tell it like it is. If you tell the children, they with their basic honesty, may tell others. By the next day the child may have shared this big "secret" with their play-mates who in turn tell their parents. This could lead to extreme embarrassment for the family. Because of these reasons the crossdresser may choose not to tell his children.

Recently I talked to a crossdresser, Betty, about the question of telling her children about crossdressing. She began by explaining to me that the children should not be burdened with trying to understand and accept her crossdressing.

Another crossdresser's wife has a different opinion.

> Our children have grown up with Fran and consider my husband's crossdressing just a part of the way our family is. They have not shared this with anyone. We did not treat it as something wierd and unusual and neither did the children.

One wife remarked to me,

> Our daughter has grown up with a father who is a crossdresser and is very openly accepting of this activity. She even asks my husband for his advice on clothing. They share certain items of feminine attire. As she got older she did tell a special friend, but this friend also is very accepting. Children who grow up in a loving, trusting relationship with their parents are able to handle these kinds of special situations. Our daughter is an example of this.

In a conversation with the 14 year old daughter of a crossdresser, she said,

> I was told that my father crossdressed when I was three years old. My parents have told me everything all of my life. This is the way it should be. I can not think of anything that would be worse than not knowing something as important as this. Think about it! We are talking about who my father is. I can not even imagine my parents not telling me.

When I asked her if she ever referred to her father by his femme name, she answered,

> No! I really don't think of him as a different person

when he is dressed. I call him "Father" regardless of his clothing. That's who he is.

The father responded,

> She and her mother are my best friends. Crossdressing has become an extension of our family, and we all three share the experience together. The only real burning issue relates to whether or not other crossdressers should come to our home enfemme. Our daughter's friends frequently come over without calling first. They know that our doors are always open, but this could cause some embarrassing moments.

I asked a crossdresser, Carmon, how the children viewed her. She explained that to the children HE was the perfect father — an all American man type.

> We ski together, go to our lake house together, and generally enjoy our family togetherness. As a man I work on cars and can repair almost anything. I don't want to destroy their image of me as a father by telling them about the crossdressing.

Carmon is very attractive when dressed as a woman. It is difficult to realize that a person who can be so feminine can also be very masculine. To the children, Carmon is Harry. The children will probably never know that Carmon exists.

Keeping crossdressing a secret is not always easy. I know several crossdressers who rent motel rooms to dress prior to organizational meetings. Some dress at home only if the children are away or in bed. I heard a funny story about the crossdresser who waits for the children's bed time. Then when the door of the crossdresser's bedroom is closed and locked he pulls out his feminine clothes. "Invariably," he said, "there is a wee voice crying out for Daddy. By this time Daddy has already been transformed."

As children get older the father's crossdressing is more likely to be discovered by the children. Meanwhile the children may become self-centered and acquire a set of their own hostilities. A common response to discover may be, "Why are you doing this to me?" or

"This is just what I need, a perverted father!" And frequently the question follows, "What will happen if my friends find out?"

I discussed these matters with my stepdaughter. In answer to the question, "Should children be told?" she answered with a very quick "NO!" She continued by saying that if children do find out, the parents should show concern for the problems faced by the children that relate either directly or indirectly to crossdressing.

In our own situation my husband's first wife had told the children in a very negative way. Shortly after we were married the matter surfaced, and we had to handle it together. There were numerous confrontations in which the negative attitudes had to be addressed. After the issue had been discussed one daughter said, "You and Dad did all the right things, so I feel pretty much O.K. about it now." Basically what we did was to show love, exercise patience, and speak honestly. It should be pointed out that the younger daughter was treated with the same patience, but to this day is totally non-accepting. Our batting average is only 50%. This proves once again that the individual personalities of children should be considered.

Patience is very important, especially during the teenage years. This may be the most difficult period for children to discover their father is a crossdresser. Teenagers usually have many unresolved issues burning within their own being, such as coping with school, peer pressures and discovering the opposite sex. They have little energy or tolerance left to face the issue of their father's crossdressing. This is also a period of the greatest physical, sociological and emotional adjustment.

In some cases after learning their father is a crossdresser, teenagers may direct hostility at their mother for putting up with the father's crossdressing and toward their father for this "unacceptable" activity. Total rejection of both parents could result. Because of the social pressures society places on young people you can not be certain that children will understand this deviation from social norms.

Attitude is crucial in how well your children deal with crossdressing. Most attitudes are developed throughout the child's life. They are the result of what the parents say and do, but also have to do with how the child processes parental guidance.

Based upon the wide diversity of attitudes presented, it should be clear that the jury is still out on the matter of telling the child about the father's crossdressing. Society may provide guidelines but not dictates. The danger, of course, is that neither the crossdresser nor his wife will want children who are total nonconformists. They don't want children who are too conforming either. Parents need to teach their children to live life with an open mind. When possible life should be approached with flexibility, and without preconceived ideas and prejudices. Children who grow up in an open situation are usually able to decide for themselves when to conform and when not to. There is no "pat" answer about how children should be handled. I would advise you to collect all possible information regarding the pros and cons of when, how, and if you should tell the children and fit this data into your own situation. Also look at the personality profile of each child. Some children will be able to handle it and some may not.

MATERNAL INSTINCTS AND THE CROSSDRESSER

I have made the point repeatedly in this book that the crossdresser is usually in touch with the better qualities of femininity. With these qualities, the crossdresser will be better prepared for parenting than most other men. The crossdresser has permitted sensitivity to surface and this carries over into the role of the parent. He is not afraid to display tenderness, or express his fears. He is more giving and compassionate.

I have observed my own husband in his role as parent. The children share their feelings openly with him. He responds with warmth and gentleness. When the children were infants he never felt out of character feeding them a bottle or changing their diaper. It is common for most crossdressers to be excellent parents. The only possible exception might be the crossdresser who is holding on to some macho behaviors in an effort to hide the feminine qualities.

Dustin Hoffman became aware of his strong nurturing quality during the filming of Kramer vs. Kramer. This was the story of an inadequate father who did not know of his inadequacies as a parent until he was placed in the position of demonstrating his ability to be a good parent. As a divorced father he was battling for the custody of his son. During this time he actually started to demonstrate maternal instincts and through the nurturing of his son became a better father. Hoffman said that during the filming he discovered a mothering instinct within him. In one scene he takes the stand during the custody hearing, and in a peak of emotion says to the judge, "Why should I not have the child? I have been a good mother!" Many crossdressers are excellent parents because they are in touch with the feelings which Hoffman described.

The majority of crossdressers I have known are individuals who are in touch with their emotions. For this reason it is advantageous for a woman to have a crossdresser as the father of her children. One wife of a crossdresser remarked, "My husband is a shining example of what a father should be. As a crossdresser he possesses the maternal instincts most men do not have."

There is one very prevalent fear that the children of crossdressers may express. The child may ask, "Will my father want to have surgery and become a real woman?" The older child may read newspaper articles or see some of the television talk shows that describe fathers who had sexual reassignment surgery. He may have fears of this happening to his father. The child may say, "Who needs two mothers?" The answer to these fears may be made clear through a published survey of heterosexual crossdressers. The survey asked this question, "Would you have surgery if you could afford the costs?" About 25% of those responding to the survey left the question open and unresolved. The people who left the issue pending, shared stories that were characterized by rejection. Most of the people in this group had no children.

One exception to this is Patsy, a transsexual. She has been married and has five sons. When I asked her why she decided to go the route of sexual reassignment surgery she described a situation in which no one in her family would accept her. Patsy felt that she could no longer continue to hide her femininity. This was like living a lie. Becoming a woman seemed to be the only way. I asked Patsy if she would have chosen surgery if her family had been understanding and accepting. Her answer was an emphatic, "No!"

When a crossdresser has the opportunity to meet other crossdressers; when a crossdresser finds love and acceptance from family and friends; when a crossdresser finds acceptance of himself — then the idea of surgery will diminish or may never occur. Those who do go the surgery route do so, in many instances, because it appears to be the only answer.

The ball is in the hands of family members. As the ball carriers you must decide to give the kind of love that will fulfill the crossdresser. If this love is present, the decision for surgery will not occur.

MY ADVICE TO CHILDREN OF CROSSDRESSERS

Children of crossdressers must realize that their family is different from other families. There are advantages and disadvantages related to these differences. They must make a strong effort to balance the negatives with the positives

The most important thing for children to remember is that while they are identified as a member of the family, they are also identified as an individual. Each person must grow within their own identity. Each person must be the best they can be individually, within the framework of their families, and within the framework of society.

There are many ways to grow. Emotional, spiritual and intellectual growth are all important. When children consider being the child of a crossdresser as a negative experience, the good news is that each person is capable of growing beyond negative influences.

If on the other hand children consider the family a positive, nurturing environment, personal growth is even more possible.

Most children need to give some thought to how they can contribute to the family. Being helpful and positive is one way. A family is at its best when each member gives as well as receives. John F. Kennedy once said, "Ask not what your country can do for you. Ask what you can do for your country."

President Kennedy learned this philosophy of sharing from being a part of a family that considered the needs of each other. Children who perceive crossdressing as a negative influence in their lives should look for ways to reach out to their father in a loving manner. It is as difficult to be a crossdresser as it is to be the child of one. Throwing off the negative attitudes will do much to help the family. Such love will open doors of joy in the present. Children should take the advice of Kennedy, and ask the question, "What can I do to make this easier for my father?"

Children should recognize the individual growth of their parents also. Crossdressers are people who have grown to the point of being in touch with both masculine and feminine components. This is what makes them unique. This is a cause for us to be glad.

MY ADVICE TO CROSSDRESSERS

My advice to the crossdresser is two fold: 1) Don't get too caught up in guilt feelings about the children. 2) Let society take some of the responsibility. It is possible that the crossdresser who feels guilt tends to superimpose guilt to the children. There is no need for guilt. If your child has reacted negatively to the fact that you are a crossdresser, simply remember that the child has his or her own identity and society contributed to that identity. If on the other hand the children of a crossdresser are open-minded and accepting there is cause to be thankful. When acceptance occurs there has been a good blend of family and societal influences, and the results are rewarding.

CASE STUDIES

The following case studies are included to help readers reach a conclusion regarding the role of crossdressers as parents. The two individual histories present opposite views.

Larry is a 16 year old son of a crossdresser. He was told of his father's crossdressing by his mother in a fit of anger. He described his reaction to me in this way.

I was 15 when I discovered that my dad is a crossdresser. He had not wanted me to know, but mother told me. My reaction moved from denial to anger, then to hurt and now I am back to denial again. When Mother told me about Dad's crossdressing I just refused to believe it. After a time of insistence she assured me that she would show me the proof of the situation. I'll never forget the moment she showed me the evidence — an assortment of women's clothing, all exactly in his size. This is when I got really mad. I was angry at him for not being honest with me, and I was mad at him for being what my mother called perverted. Somehow I consider the omission of truth to be a form of dishonesty, and I consider doing something so contrary to society absolutely uncalled for.

I am trying to understand what's going on. I feel hurt because I've always been very close to my father. He has been my idol for as long as I can remember. He was everything masculinity is suppose to be in its more perfect form. I must have come full circle, because I'm back to denial. Thoughts about my father's crossdressing are usually repressed and obscured. I find this matter best handled in a situation where it is not talked about much. I am aware that no person is perfect, but from my point of view crossdressing is my dad's fault. The main thing I know is that I am responsible for my own life, and a part of that responsibility will relate to sorting out influences from my parents and from society.

It appears that Larry's initial reaction related to the fact that he was told in a way that causes a negative shadow upon the father and upon the act of crossdressing. Children are taught to believe their parents, and Larry's mother had said that crossdressing is perverted. She also described his father as having some type of moral corruption.

Since Larry has been taught by his father to take responsibility for his own life, it is possible that he will come to a level of acceptance in time. It will not be easy for Larry, because the parents did not act as a team in the matter. Larry was placed in a no win situation, because regardless of his position he is forced to go against one of his parents. It was easier initially to accept the mother's views, because she had society on her side.

In the following case study Lydia, age 13, describes her life as the daughter of a crossdresser.

> My father is a crossdresser and I think this is fantastic. My sister, age 16, Mom, Dad, and I all share clothing. We have a lot of fun. Sometimes when I'm out with my dad when he is dressed as a woman I forget and call him DAD. This has created some embarrassing moments for us all, but we usually just laugh it off. I love my dad. It is wonderful sharing all these things with him. I'd have it no other way. Dad is a pilot and teaches others to fly. Sometimes he dresses as a woman and teaches the classes. The students think Rebecca is Dad's sister. They say Rebecca is much nicer than Dad. I agree. I really like Rebecca a lot. When I grow up I want to be just like Rebecca.

Several things characterize Lydia's family. They are open and loving. They have fun and they are able to laugh at themselves even when a situation is embarrassing. Both the mother and father agreed upon how and when the children should be told. This family does things together and they share. Because of these factors accepting crossdressing was really not a big issue. It was in fact a fun part of their lives.

SELF-AFFIRMATION

Crossdressers and their families should take time to establish what is called "a self-affirmation." The statements below, adapted from Transactional Analysis, could start you in the direction of formulating your own list. Think about them, live them, then guide your children in the formulation of their own ideas.

1. I am solely responsible for my own life and well-being. If I am not happy and at peace with myself it is up to me to discover the causes and take the appropriate action. Others may help me, but I am ultimately responsible for my inner self.

2. I have the innate authority to take full charge of my life.

3. There is a price exacted for everything I do. It is up to me to determine such price and intelligently decide whether or not I am able and willing to pay it.

4. I am inescapably responsible for everything I do, for I inevitably benefit or suffer according to the consequences of my every act.

5. I have the right and freedom to make mistakes, to be defeated and to fail.

6. My wishes are determined by my awareness.

7. All "oughts" "shoulds" and "musts" are irrelevant and meaningless for any action without inner motivation.

8. I must do the best I can possibly do at the time.

9. If I have done my best there is no valid justification for self-condemnation. I will be free of any self-imposed shame, guilt or remorse.

10. Life is a series of decisions that can be described as either wise or unwise.

11. We must pay a "price" for our every unwise decision.

12. There is no valid basis for resisting anything that can not be changed. Things that can not be changed, i.e., crossdressing, should be accepted.

13. I can consciously increase my awareness by desiring to improve it, and by sharing with others.

14. I realize that worry, resistance and resentment are both futile and destructive to one's well-being.

15. I am the center of my universe, therefore the quality of my world will relate directly to my own quality.

16. I am the most important, interesting and challenging person in my life.

17. My fundamental responsibility in life is to increase my understanding of life and the lives of those around me, i.e., the crossdresser.

18. I am a genuine "success" to the degree that I feel warm and loving toward myself and others.

19. My mistakes can contribute to my learning and growth.

20. I can be limited only by the degree of my knowledge.

21. To be motivated I must perceive desirable benefits arising from the proposed action.

22. To be widely motivated I must determine my real need, the anticipated benefits available, the total price demanded for each, and whether or not I am able and willing to pay it.

23. My physical well-being is of critical importance to my emotional well-being.

24. My mind is like a computer that receives and evaluates information, but I am much more than a computer because of my five senses, intuition and spirit.

25. I am a unique and precious being, inviolable, invincible and eternal, ever doing the best I can, growing in wisdom and love.

HELPING THE FAMILY WIN

It is important that the entire family take on the stance of winners. To do this each person must think like a winner and act like a winner. This will help the wife and the children as they attempt to accept DAD as he is.

WINNERS

Help others to be winners.

Record your wins.

Make winning plans.

Have a minimum of ten wants.

Have many interests.

Have many options.

Accept others.

Do — Don't try.

Plan for emergencies.

Set priorities.

Prepare for possible separations from loved ones.

Give many strokes.

Learn from mistakes.

Think about winning.

Congratulate yourself for winning - accept it.

Know when you aren't you.

Live in the present.

Know that you are not perfect.

Smile from within.

LOSERS

Live in the past.

Have old standards of good and bad.

Are predictable.

Are manipulated easily.

Give automatic responses.

Are safe but miserable.

Are preoccupied with internal dialogue.

Are not aware of the needs of others.

Do not believe it is necessary to give others strokes.

Feel under pressure continually.

Can't say no to anyone or themselves.

Ask continually, "How am I doing?"

Do not listen to others.

Are overextended — promise a lot and rarely deliver.

Are lonely.

Overindulge in eating, smoking or drinking.

Feel that happiness is for others — not themselves.

Can't ask anyone for anything.

Don't trust easily.

Are indecisive.

Have difficulty being real.

Avoid intimacy.

Relive most of their past mistakes.

Avoid honesty.

Expect to lose.

THINGS LOSERS TELL THEMSELVES:

You don't deserve it.

You'll pay for it.

You won't make it.

You'll never get it.

Don't be who you are.

Don't get close.

You'll regret it.

Don't grow up.

Don't, Don't, Don't!

Losers are seldom flexible enough to accept the crossdresser. Winners are secure enough to demonstrate acceptance. Read the list and make your choice!

CHAPTER NINE

THE EFFECTS OF SUPPRESSED FEMININITY

Mark Twain once said, "At age twelve a boy starts to imitate a man, and he continues to do that for the rest of his life." We see this imitation of masculinity all the time. Athletes have a power handshake. Football players throw the football vigorously toward the ground after a touchdown. Tennis players become famous for profanity on the court. Men, including some crossdressers, go to extremes to prove to the world that they are all man. In a true masculine spirit they say, "Winning isn't everything. It is the only thing."

With drive and determination they face the world. Many of the joys of life are missed along the way. They miss the pleasure of their own inherent gentility. Frequently success is equated with professional achievement rather than personal fulfillment. Sometimes affection is lost, because once caught up in the drama of acting like men, the drama itself becomes the driving force of their lives. When this happens self-interest and individuality are more important than the development of relationships. As the following poem indicates these men think mainly of self.

> I like the way I walk.
> I like the way I talk.
> Honey, if you don't like my style,
> I'll never sit and stay awhile.

The irony here is that many women enjoy this demonstration of masculinity. The preference for macho goes back to primitive times when strong men defended the honor of their women. They believed the tough, bold brute could protect his family best. Women feel secure if they know their honor will always be safe. Husbands are dedicated to keeping the little woman happy, so they continue to act out the role assigned to men. For crossdressers this is an especially difficult role to fill, because they have such a large feminine side of their personalities.

When the crossdresser becomes secure with his true nature there will be less of a tendency toward the outward demonstration of macho behavior. He will no longer feel it necessary to roll up the shirt sleeves to show off his tatoos.

BREAKING AWAY FROM MACHO

Sometimes men are so caught up in the masculine role that any discovery of feminine qualities occurs quite by accident. This was the case of Harry, who served the armed services abroad.

I found myself associating with the nurses who were assigned to our division. In the evenings after a long day they would slip into some comfortable lounging clothes and sit on their beds for girl talk. They never thought of me as an intruder. I was just one of the girls. Soon I began to feel out of place in my starched military clothing. When the girls sensed my discomfort they offered me a robe to wear. The robe seemed to put me into a feminine mood. It was such a nice release from the pressures. Before long the girls started calling me Sally.

When Sally got into the feminine role a kinder more gentle side emerged. The nurses were the catalyst for the breaking away from macho. Once Harry had experienced the joy of femininity he became a crossdresser for life. It is very possible that these feelings had always been a part of Harry, but he had never permitted them to surface. He was too busy acting like a man; he was the he-man who didn't take guff from the girls.

FUSING THE GENDER ROLES

Frequently it is a woman who helps a man discover the feminine side of the personality. In Harry's case it was the nurses. For many crossdressers the female love figure is their mother. Soft clothing may stir memories of the warmth and nurturing received when they were young.

The poet, Novalis, describes his experience of finding both masculine and feminine qualities fused within his life.

Born with the hardness of character, my intellect was expanded until the heart was removed from its domain. It was Sophie that returned my heart to its legitimate throne.

After meeting Sophie, Novalis recognized that the masculine and feminine sides were both present in his psyche. He decided to express the feminine qualities within his life. He knew that to resist these qualities meant that he would be less than whole and less than human.

THE LOVE OF FEMININITY

As a group crossdressers seem to instinctively know how to love femininity. The association with an exemplary female is frequently the joy of their lives. When they move to a conscious understanding of this love of femininity, they also move to the more tangible expression of it. They demonstrate what they feel with clothing. Dressing as a woman helps them stay in touch with the feelings and emotions usually associated with femininity.

The real test of a man is whether or not he is able to be himself. Femininity is a very real and dynamic part of the crossdresser. When he becomes secure in his identity there will be less desire to act macho. The true feminine feelings will emerge. He will no longer be threatened nor challenged by other men. From beneath the tough talk and brute swagger will emerge a security great enough to show feminine qualities.

For my husband his feminine side, Melanie, unlocks an emotional, caring side. He is not afraid to show the depth of his love. Now that I have adjusted to the idea of his crossdressing, it seems that Melanie adds dimension to our relationship.

Dustin Hoffman felt that the role of Dorothy added the same kind of dimension to his life. In the movie, Tootsie, Hoffman played Michael Dorsey, a well-respected but seldom employed New York stage actor. The story describes Michael, who auditions for the role of Dorothy in a television soap opera. Much to his surprise he gets the part. The role opens up a whole new area of life for Michael Dorsey. What is even more significant is that playing the part of a woman opened up a new area of feelings for Hoffman. As an actor Hoffman got into the heart of the character, Dorothy. This kind of artistic empathy won him an Academy Award, but even more important, it won him the rich experience of being Dorothy. The feeling turned out to be a very positive experience, because the transformation that changed Hoffman into Dorothy brought a rare kind of pleasure.

Hoffman is very interested in exploring his feminine side. This interest actually began with the movie Kramer vs. Kramer. In this movie he felt the joys of motherhood. Through these experiences he has concluded that gender is not as polarized as society dictates that it should be. Hoffman desired another opportunity to explore the newly discovered feelings of femininity. Following Kramer vs. Kramer he became obsessed with the idea of putting together another movie in which he could move away from the masculine life script. Hoffman collaborated with script writers and producers to create the movie, Tootsie. While Tootsie is a light movie it does clearly show that a man gains precious insight by viewing the world through the eyes of a woman.

WHY DO MEN BECOME CROSSDRESSERS?

I believe that men become crossdressers because they are born with some feminine qualities. My husband has said that the clothes provide a stage on which these feminine qualities can be expressed. Feminine clothing is used as a tool by crossdressers for four reasons. Two of these can be described as feminine needs, while the other two relate to the need to find relief from masculine role expectancies.

THE NEED TO EXPERIENCE BEAUTY AND ACQUIRE VIRTUE

Lets face it, men don't feel very pretty in a business suit. While in the animal world the male is the creature of beauty this is not the case with humans. Women are considered to be the creatures of beauty. Men are sometimes the ones who provide the beautiful clothing for their women. Womanhood has become the repository of all that is good, desirable and virtuous. Through clothing crossdressers can symbolically experience this goodness and this beauty.

THE NEED FOR PERSONALITY EXPRESSION

Crossdressers have the confidence to recognize the feminine qualities within their personality, but they find it very difficult to express softness while wearing the coarse, heavy, clothing assigned to men within our society. It is much easier to feel feminine when wearing Brussel's Lace and Chanel No. 5.

Men must do as Mark Twain said they would do. They act like men, but there is a time when enough is enough. The feminine side must emerge, and usually it emerges wearing a dress.

RELIEF FROM THE REQUIREMENTS OF MASCULINITY

Masculinity is forceful, aggressive and virile. Men prove how tough they are. Within our minds there is an imaginary essence of what a man should be. Masculinity is rigid, and those who loudly acclaim how much of it they possess want to steer clear of any hint of emotionally charged femininity. Crossdressers, on the other hand, want to be relieved of masculinity. They have been expected to be something that they have little interest in being -all man. In one respect it is necessary. They may want to earn a promotion so that they can provide well for their families, but for the crossdresser there is more to life than work. There is certainly more to life than masculine life scripts.

Frequently the wives of crossdressers will say, "Why don't you take up stamp collecting if you want a hobby?" The truth is, crossdressing is definitely not a hobby. It is the expression of a part of the personality. Golf, hunting, baseball, fast cars, or fast women will not take away the need to express femininity. Crossdressing is the greatest relief from the pressures of a man's world.

RELIEF FROM BEING WHAT OTHERS EXPECT

There has been a lot written about the new male image. Today men have been relieved from some previously dictated role expectations, but some of these expectations are still very much a part of our ideas about what men should do. Basically men are still the provider and protector. Their responsibilities for the care and feeding of the family are still active. Men still have to "live up to" our expectations. For the crossdresser, there is escape from these things through clothing and by assuming a feminine personality.

WHY DO SOME MEN SUPPRESS CROSSDRESSING?

There are three reasons men sometimes decide to suppress crossdressing:

1. There is a feeling that crossdressing is wrong.

2. There is a fear of feminine traits and qualities.

3. Wives and others prefer that they not crossdress.

Regardless of the reason, the crossdresser will not be successful in his efforts to suppress femininity for a very long period of time. All crossdressers that I have talked with have described one or more of these reasons for an attempted purging. Somewhere and sometime in the future, the desire will surface again. During the times in which the desire is suppressed, there could be some manifestations of psychological or physiological disorders. It is as if their body is crying out to be freed of the suppression. During these times their lives have little direction. In many cases there may also be depression.

Crossdressers should not be expected to hide a part of their true identity. Rather they should go through what I consider the five steps toward fulfillment.

1. The crossdresser should learn to accept himself without remorse or guilt.

2. The crossdresser should handle or dissipate fear.

3. He should gamble on love; tell the loved one about the need to crossdress.

4. He should patiently wait for the acceptance from the loved one.

5. The crossdresser should work on feeling secure within a social frame of reference.

CHAPTER TEN

GETTING PROFESSIONAL HELP

Here is a riddle for you:

How many psychologists does it take to change a light bulb?

Answer:

It only takes one psychologist to change a light bulb unless the bulb is stuck in the socket. When a light bulb is stuck in the socket all the psychologists in the world can not remove it. If they try the bulb will shatter into thousands of pieces. To quote a nursery rhyme, "All the king's horses and all the king's men can never put it together again."

So it is with crossdressers. One psychologist can provide therapy for most human problems, but the crossdresser can not be cured from crossdressing. It really does not matter how many psychologists are employed to attempt a "cure." Crossdressing can not be cured. When professionals try to treat the crossdresser the result is not that different from the light bulb. The crossdresser may shatter into a thousand pieces.

WHAT ARE THE OPTIONS?

This riddle and human application is probably not what crossdressers and their loved ones wanted to hear. I know hundreds of crossdressers who would love to go to a psychologist and get "fixed." The family members would like that also. The crossdresser's only choice is to seek help for the purpose of accepting himself as he is rather than what others want him to be. It could be beneficial for the crossdresser to know that crossdressing is not, nor ever has been, a fatal disease. The options relate to choosing the best professional who can offer the greatest insight into the nature of crossdressing.

Psychiatrists are medical doctors who have specialized in psychiatry, the study and treatment of mental disorders. They are highly trained, medical specialists. Since crossdressing is not a mental disorder it is doubtful that a psychiatrist would be the most valuable resource for the crossdresser seeking counseling. It is also doubtful that the psychiatrist would consider the crossdresser in need of therapy unless there were other evident psychiatric problems.

A **psychologist** will have either a Ph.D, Doctor of Philosophy, or an Ed.D, Doctor of Education, degree. While these professionals do not have a medical degree, they will always have extensive training in psychopathology. The field of psychology examines the reasons why people think, act and feel the way they do. Psychology analyzes mental processes in the same way sociology analyzes social processes. I know many crossdressers who have been helped by psychologists. Some crossdressers need guidance if they are to understand the dynamics of crossdressing. With professional help crossdressers can gain insight into their own self-identity. Researcher Gaetano Benedetti stated that the personality of most crossdressers is characterized by a struggle for self-identity. I believe this is true, therefore helping the crossdresser come to grips with who he really is will probably represent one major contribution by the psychologist or any other helping professional.

A **psychoanalyst** employs the technical methods of Sigmund Freud. These professionals will have either a master's or doctoral degree in psychiatry, psychology or social work. Psychoanalysts are skilled in the art of analyzing the human mind in an effort to find specific causes for behavior patterns.

There are professionals within each of these groups who could provide valuable insight for the crossdresser. Unfortunately there are also professionals who know little or nothing about the etiology of crossdressing. Since the subject and the dynamics of crossdressing are so new within the behavioral science fields many professionals do not have the knowledge and skills to provide help for the crossdresser. For this reason the greatest help may come from other crossdressers rather than from a helping professional. Crossdressers may find it valuable to share experiences with each other. Sometimes the other crossdressers are the best to recommend a helping professional when one is needed, because they will know better than anyone which helping professionals have the knowledge and skills to provide counseling to the crossdresser and his family or significant others.

The most important thing to remember is that no crossdresser has ever been permanently "cured." This would be as difficult as being "cured" of blue eyes, short legs or freckles. The only "cure" that can be offered by a helping professional is providing understanding and guidance that will lead the crossdresser in the direction of self-realization and self-acceptance.

WHAT ARE THE CAUSES?

If the crossdresser decides to seek counseling from a helping professional, one of the first questions he may ask the professional is, "Why am I a crossdresser? What causes me to want to crossdress?" The answer the crossdresser may receive to these questions will probably depend upon the professional. Every professional seems to have his/her own theory. None of the numerous theories explaining crossdressing have been proven. Very little research has been conducted on the subject of crossdressing because mental health researchers are more concerned with finding cures for mental illness. Crossdressing is not considered a mental illness. Mental health professionals for the most part do not consider crossdressing a problem beyond the reality that crossdressers are not understood or accepted by society. Within this decade there has been increased interest by helping professionals and the general public regarding crossdressing. Television interview programs such as Donahue and Geraldo have attempted to address the topic, and professional journals have presented articles and data. In many cases the information presented is insignificant from a statistical point of view. For example one research study noted that 05% of all crossdressers had a closer relationship with their mother, and she wanted a daughter instead of a son. Five percentage points is not significant enough to establish a theory of causation. We could just as easily say that 05% of all crossdressers had a rabbit for a pet at some time in their life. Could we then conclude that having rabbits for pets causes a boy to become a crossdresser? No! I hardly think this would represent sound research.

Other research has noted that there is no significant difference between the **hormonal profile** of crossdressers and that of the general male population.

The Journal of the American Psychoanalytic Association presented a related idea. In an article by Ethel Person, the fantasies of crossdressers were described. According to Person the cross dresser attempts to disassociate himself from the masculine part of his personality through fantasy. She called the fantasy a **lesbian preoccupation**. Person feels that the preoccupation is caused by a discomfort with the masculine gender role. She noted that most crossdressers have this need to escape from their masculinity. Through wearing the clothing of the opposite sex and expressing their inner feelings of femininity, they achieve this escape. Crossdressers are told by society that they are to act, dress, think and look like men and not women. The only problem with this is that crossdressers at certain times want to dress, think and feel like women. They have a need to express femininity at least a part of the time. The amount of time varies among crossdressers. I have been amused when I observe some crossdressers who grow tired of the role at times. For example Susan attended a weekend planned activity with us recently. She rode in our car fully dressed as Sue. After a weekend of dressing as a woman, her feet were killing her and she seemed anxious to get back home to the routine of wearing a business suit, starched shirt and comfortable shoes.

Other theorists have suggested that crossdressing has either **biological** or **genetic causes**. The **chromosome push theory** contends that the developing embryo is sexually undifferentiated for the first six weeks. At that time the male Y chromosome "pushes" the gonads to become testes, which then regulate the hormone formula to develop the male genital tract. This "push" is supposedly weaker than normal, in crossdressers.

Other researchers feel that as newborns all human beings have the behavioral aspects of both sexes. Within moments of his birth, however, a little boy's parents effectively punch the **blue button** on the social computer within his head. This starts an imaginary program that society has deemed is appropriate for a "proper boy." He is protected from, and punished for, any manifestation of softness, empathy or femininity.

Behavioral researchers also theorize that all people have facets of both masculinity and femininity within their personalities. The only real difference between crossdressers and other males is that the crossdresser **acknowledges his feminine side** and has discovered a feeling of completeness previously missing.

I have had at least one crossdresser tell me that he believes in the **reincarnation theory**. While in a hypnotic trance he saw himself in his previous life as a woman. He said that he clearly saw the town where he lived during the other life. Convinced that this was true, the crossdresser took a trip to New Orleans for the purpose of finding the house where he lived as beautiful Christine, who died at an early age from child birth. Apparently Christine's spirit longed for another life and came back as a part of my friend. This was his theory to explain his crossdressing. Many people do not agree with this.

Prenatal symbiotic fusion is another theory several researchers have suggested to explain the cause for crossdressing. According to this theory there is locked in the crossdresser's subconscious memory the pleasures of the prenatal state. The expressions of femininity help them capture the feelings they experienced in the wonderful warm, moist environment of their mother's womb.

Other crossdressers feel that they were **destined** to be crossdressers. In other cases the **role model of the father** is mentioned as a related cause. I know several crossdressers who say that they never really felt close to their fathers. The irony here is that I know just as many who tell of a strong **paternal bonding**. In the search for an explanation the most common statement could go something like this, "I don't know why I am a crossdresser. There are so many theories that it gets confusing."

WHAT CROSSDRESSERS SHOULD UNDERSTAND

There are some things that crossdressers should know about themselves. They do not need a professional to tell them. They may, however, need a professional to help them adjust to these truths. For one thing they know that as crossdressers they, "March to the beat of a different drummer." Whether they are out of step with society or society is out of step with them does not really matter. They are different, and they know it. The presence of a very large feminine side sets them apart from other men. Again it could be that the rest of the male population has the same feminine inclination but fails to recognize this part of their personalities. Crossdressers really don't expect acceptance from the total population. They do hope for, and in some cases even pray for, the acceptance from those they love the most. Their own emotional distress is almost totally related to a lack of acceptance from their loved ones. All crossdressers that have experienced a strong rejection have tried to "cure themselves." Most crossdressers I have talked with have admitted that these cures were short lived. The need to crossdress and express the feminine side returns.

Crossdressers know that there is no "cure." For this reason the wife who says,"If you love me, you will give this up," is making a futile and unrealistic plea. He may love her with all his heart, but he can not give up crossdressing. This would be like saying,"If you love me you would give up your mind, soul and heart." This example is a little extreme, because giving up vital organs would mean sudden death. Giving up a part of the personality causes death also, but the death is very slow and very painful.

THE LAST SECRET

A crossdresser, Krystal, described for me the heartaches she felt as she attempted to find a "cure" for her crossdressing.

I have lived all of my life feeling that I am less than a man, and less than normal. As a young man I did all the normal things such as participating in sports, dating girls and even getting married. For me marriage represented my last testimonial to my personal masculinity. I prayed to God that marriage would deliver me from the deep despair of rejection. There was even the hope that being married would take away the need to crossdress. I guess I thought that one pleasure could be substituted for another. At the time of our marriage my new bride knew most things about me. She knew that I liked sausage with my egg, I enjoyed candle light with dinner, and blue was my favorite color. Since I really wanted the crossdressing to go away, it was never mentioned before marriage. As it turned out, marriage was not a cure for crossdressing. Our marriage was built upon Christian principles including honesty, but when I withheld the truth about crossdressing, I was far from honest. Soon I needed to examine my heart in this matter. My wife was truly a wonderful person, and I loved her with my whole heart. I lacked the courage needed to tell her for a long time. To put it bluntly I lied to her. I would say that I was going to visit my mother, and would go to a motel where I could dress.

Through the years the guilt grew to a point that was unbearable. Looking back I acted in an impulsive manner when I actually did tell her. She got the truth with no background information to make the truth more bearable. She rejected me because of crossdressing. She would say, "Don't touch me. Don't even come near me." I felt lonely, isolated and full of despair.

We went through a long series of counseling sessions. The psychologist that was working with us did not tell her what she wanted to hear. He told us that while the practice of crossdressing is different from the norm it really isn't harmful to anyone. There were other times that the counselor knew less about crossdressing than I did.

I have wondered many times what would have happened if we had worked this out before marriage. To tell you the truth I don't believe she would have married me. We are still in marriage counseling, and our relationship has improved some. Perhaps the best thing that has come from these sessions has been my own self-awareness. I have also grown in my ability to accept rejection. Now I can say, "Here I am. This is who I am. Accept me or reject me. I can never change." I have won a few battles, but there is still a war. Perhaps with the help of our counselor, with the help from God, and the help from my wife, we will someday work everything out.

Krystal is only one of perhaps as many as fifteen million men in this country who are heterosexual male crossdressers. Each has his own unique and often tragic story to tell. Finding an understanding, knowledgeable, helping professional who can provide counseling for the crossdresser is difficult. For many crossdressers the only help they find is through crossdressing organizations. The last chapter describes help available through crossdressing organizations and their addresses.

CHAPTER ELEVEN

LEARNING TO LOVE YOUR HUSBAND ENFEMME

When a male crossdresser assumes his feminine personality and wears female clothing he is said to be **enfemme**. It would be wrong to consider this as role playing. The crossdresser wants to be perceived as a woman. What is even more important, he wants to be loved as a woman. This is a tall order for the wife who has just discovered her husband's need to crossdress. She feels anxiety, fear, confusion and sometimes disgust.

Fear of not being accepted and loved is very strong for the crossdresser. As a heterosexual male he will probably desire a love relationship with a wife or girl friend. Most crossdressers have a need to share their femmeself with the love of their life, but some very real questions emerge. What will her reaction be? How will she cope with having a "sister" for a lover? How will she perceive the large feminine component within the personality of the person she loves? Her attitude is probably not that different from the attitudes of society in general. Initially she may be far from accepting. The crossdresser will know that the response is not positive. This form of rejection is the most crippling obstacle a crossdresser must face. Overcoming her own negative emotions will be the greatest hurdle for the woman in the crossdresser's life. Once she sees the pain caused by rejection there could be an effort directed toward accepting her husband and then going on toward her ultimate goal of loving him enfemme.

Once the husband has openly communicated that he is not gay, emotionally disturbed, or transsexual the two of them will be in a position to work on some compromises and deal with the negative emotions. It should be evident to the wife that her husband is still the same person she married. The acceptance of the wife is vital if her husband is to be complete as a person.

DEAL WITH YOUR EMOTIONS FIRST

The wife who has not faced her own emotions will not be able to help her husband. She may not be able to love the visible expressions of her husband's feminine side. It is highly possible that she already loves the feminine personality traits that motivate the crossdressing, but it is normal to feel uncertain and anxious about him actually "putting on the clothing." These feelings must be discussed openly. Before the wife can deal with her husband's needs she must feel that her own needs have been met. It is obvious that there are many issues that must be addressed. Hopefully she will not waste too much time drowned in negative feelings of anger and hostility. To say that these are self-defeating emotions would be putting it mildly. These unhealthy feelings are bad for both the crossdresser and his wife. I think it is best to admit these feelings, deal with them, and then if possible put them to rest. It might also help if the crossdresser confirmed that the wife or girl friend has every logical reason to feel as she does. These emotions must be sorted out before she can overcome negative responses and start loving all aspects of her husband's life. What are some of the emotions that typically follow being told about crossdressing?

Loneliness is one of the first emotion felt by the wife. Not only does she feel that she's "the only tin can in the dump," she finds the symbolic "dump" a lonely place to be. Who can she talk to about this problem? I really thought that I could talk with my sister, but talking with her about this matter turned out to be a mistake. She had the same conservative social conditioning that I did. Without the strong love that I felt for Mel it was impossible for her to move past the level of tolerance. She didn't even begin to understand. I couldn't talk to Mel's parents, because they were still in a state of denial about the whole thing. On the rare occasions when I mustered up the courage to discuss it with them they very quickly changed the subject. Sometimes they actually said, "We really don't want to discuss this." The crossdresser is about the only person who can share the secret initially. Sometimes his own insight is lacking, and sometimes solidity of the relationship is lacking. Because of this the conversations may not be as fulfilling as they should be.

Many wives feel **betrayed**. In some cases in which the husband waited a long time to share the information about crossdressing, the wife feels that he has withheld a very large portion of himself. Other wives have said that they feel betrayed sexually. In our relationship this was true. Once Melanie moved in there has been no love making with Mel. I am not even sure Mel is capable of making love without the presence of Melanie. Sexually the person that I married IS Melanie. Discovering that I would be making love to Melanie was what the big shock actually was all about. For many couples this is not a problem because the femmeself is not involved in love making except in the fantasies of the crossdresser. In some cases in which the femmeself is involved in love making, the wives have opted to withdraw from sex altogether. I personally think that this is a mistake. Any negative bargaining over the bed or over the table is fatal to the marriage.

Fear is a common emotion in this situation. It is human nature to fear the unknown. We do not understand enough about crossdressing in the beginning. We don't even know our husband enfemme. When fear enters into the picture the best antidote is open communication. The husband can put many of the fears to rest. He can reassure his wife in matters of his own sexual preference. He is not gay. He is not wearing feminine clothing in order to attract other men. As a matter of fact he is the exact opposite to the drag queen. He is a femmophile, a lover of the feminine. Nor will the clothing be worn as a mockery of women. He loves femininity too much. The crossdresser will not wear the clothing for laughs either. This is not a laughing matter for the crossdressers that I know. In no way can a crossdresser be considered a sexual pervert.

At first wives tend to fear that their husbands are transsexuals. There has been a lot of publicity about sexual reassignment surgery. This is a valid fear. I personally would find no pleasure in being married to another woman. Some crossdressers decide to live their life as women without going the surgical route. This idea arouses less fear than the surgical route, but it still causes anxiety. She can picture life with no more romantic dinner dances and no more nights out with the man of her life. This fear should be openly discussed.

Selfishness is an emotion that wives and husbands must deal with. How much of the family money should be spent on "HER" wardrobe? How much of the couple's time must be shared with the husband's feminine side? Selfishness is not a negative trait limited to the wives. Sometimes crossdressers put crossdressing ahead of the wife. Generosity is a positive replacement. Both the husband and wife must be willing to give a little, to compromise and think of the other person's needs. The interesting point here is that as the crossdresser is permitted to spend more time "enfemme" many of the negative masculine traits will be replaced with positive feminine traits. The wife may find the idea which she previously feared will bring a bonus into their lives.

HELP HIM FEEL NORMAL

Once all the wife's emotional reactions to crossdressing have been openly discussed, the wife is in a better position to reach out to her husband. Each of them must be able to express what their specific needs are. Frequently until the emotional problems are resolved they may not even know what these needs are. It is the wife who can help the husband unscramble fears and anxieties. She should realize that his problem is more societal than personal. The wife should notice the pain and agony felt by her husband. Society has inflicted crossdressers with an unfair amount of guilt, shame, anxiety and disenchantment. For the crossdresser fear has become a way of life. He needs to feel a harmony with society. He needs to feel good about himself. He needs to feel NORMAL. Once these things have been accomplished the crossdresser can lead a happy life, but it is vital that he stay in touch with the masculine side and the feminine side of the personality. There should be no guilt associated with this personality integration.

HELP HIM FEEL SUCCESSFUL AS A MAN

Sometimes in the effort to help the crossdresser get in touch with his feminine side we forget that the masculine side of the personality must also be expressed. Many crossdressers are very successful as men. I know crossdressers who are pilots, accountants, physicians, psychologists and geophysicists. Many are highly successful professionals. These men are intelligent and task centered. The wife can assist her husband by being supportive of his career and the demands that the career may make upon him. Most crossdressers will find pleasure in both masculinity and femininity. For many crossdressers being feminine is a good release from the pressures felt on the job. Because of this, being enfemme helps him be more successful as a man. Behavioral science has found that all persons have both masculine and feminine traits within their personality. It is the crossdresser who has capitalized upon this human advantage.

HELP HIM CRYSTALIZE THE FEMININE SIDE OF THE PERSONALITY

Much of the professional literature about crossdressing calls it a gender dysphoria. The literal meaning of this is "to feel ill at ease." If the researchers knew crossdressers they would coin a new description. Crossdressers are very comfortable with their feminine side. It is only when society or family resist the feminine qualities that the crossdressers feel ill at ease. Even then the feeling is directed toward the people who resist them not toward the tendency to be a crossdresser. The wife can help the crossdresser crystalize the feminine personality by permitting HIM to become a HER. That sounds like a lot of double talk, but that is what all of this is about. When enfemme the cross dresser wants to be called by the feminine name and referred to as HER, SHE, etc. At first this is a very difficult thing for the wife to do. She married a man, and in most respects it is difficult to see HIM as a HER.

When the feminine side of the personality has emerged completely the crossdresser starts to feel like a complete person. During the time of adjustment there was probably a conflict between the masculine and feminine components. External forces that include both the family and society have the power to thwart the growth of the crossdresser's feminine personality. This greatly affects his feelings of harmony and contentment. These forces send out the message that the very existence of a dynamic feminine side causes the crossdresser to be living a lie. This is sometimes labeled a moral issue. Many wives look to areas of morality to defend their position that their husband is wrong. At the point of acceptance the wife will start to look for what is RIGHT about it. This will give the crossdresser the license to crystalize the feminine personality.

LOVE HIM

Love is a basic part of the human life. It is as vital as food, water and sleep. What kind of love does the crossdresser need? The ideal love is described in 1 Corinthians:13.

"Love suffers long and is kind."

This scripture verse is saying that a person can hurt a little and still be kind. It is possible to smile when you feel pain. If you love someone the love will endure. Families of crossdressers have suffered. This is a reality. Ideally the love is greater than the suffering.

"Love does not envy, does not vault itself up, and is not puffed up."

I have heard about wives who do not want their husbands to look pretty. The wife has been on a pedestal all alone, and she doesn't want to share the vaulted position. Some wives feel envy when the husband walks out of the closet looking as pretty as she does. On the other hand I think wives deserve as many pretty dresses as the crossdresser. This should be a matter of sharing. True love makes room for the other person to have honor. In a love relationship we should want the best for each other.

"Love does not behave unseemly, seeketh not its own way, is not easily provoked, and does not think evil."

Many families scream a lot. They behave unseemly. It becomes evident that each person is thinking only of their own self-interest. The energies are directed toward meeting their own needs.

For love to be complete each person must expand their world to include others. As the wife adjusts to the idea of the cross-dressing she will probably be provoked less. During the adjustment period the crossdresser must be patient and kind. Wives should waste no time with thoughts of their husband in a homosexual relationship. This will not happen. It is healthy to keep these "fears" out of the mind because they are destructive.

"Love does not rejoice in wrong or iniquity, but love rejoices in truth."

The energy of the crossdresser and his wife should be directed toward discovering the truth about each other and about the phenomenon of crossdressing. Read as much as you can about the subject. One word of caution. Read with an open mind. There is a lot of printed material that is not accurate. People have written about crossdressing only because it seemed like an interesting dissertation topic. In many cases the crossdresser will instinctively know which articles are true. They can confirm the truth of their own feelings with other crossdressers.

"Love bears all things, hopes for all things and endures all things."

Early after finding out that my husband was a crossdresser I told him that our love was greater than any problem that could enter our lives. I'll be the first to admit that there were times when it took all the energy we could muster up to live by this statement. We can look back now and say that our love really is greater than all problems. My husband has told me that finding love and total acceptance has been the highest point of his entire life. Seeing him find this kind of fulfillment has given me an equivalent joy. We believe in each other. We have hope.

"Love never fails."

This is the strongest statement in the entire passage of scripture. The love of God and the love of family together will be victorious over all odds. Loving the crossdresser enfemme is the ultimate goal.

CHAPTER TWELVE

HELP FROM ORGANIZATIONS

Sometimes organizations for crossdressers are called sororities without women. This is only partially true. Wives of crossdressers are an important part of the organizations. Mature wives assist their husbands fill leadership roles. They also provide guidance for other wives who are trying to understand. One crossdresser expressed the value of the wives group in this way,

> We are now fortunate to have in our chapter a wives' group which provides my wife with peers she can talk with. This group has helped, for now she knows that she doesn't have to bear the situation alone.

Through membership wives can come to see that their husband is a part of a misunderstood minority. They will also be able to see the results of prejudices that have been hurled at them by society. The organization becomes a support group in which these issues can be openly discussed. People need people. Crossdressers are no different. Frequently it is not possible to venture out into "the real world," but going out to meetings provides an outlet. Interaction with others is valuable for the peace of mind both of the crossdresser and his wife. The crossdresser gains self-acceptance and self-understanding. Wives profit from interaction. Everyone walks away from the meetings feeling better about crossdressing, at least this is the goal. Few people can overcome guilt and anxiety without the help of others. The emerging crossdresser and his wife will benefit from friendship with those who have already advanced to the point of accepting the feminine personality. Compassion, support and encouragement are all by-products of the organizations.

Most organizations have an active outreach program. Correspondence with people who are seeking information about crossdressing is conducted on a daily basis. There are also numerous publications available. These will present the outlook of helping professionals, present case studies of crossdressers, and address many of the concerns and issues related to crossdressing. The telephone is a valuable tool also. Sometimes wives are afraid and apprehensive. A telephone is a safe way to get help.

WHY WIVES ARE AFRAID TO JOIN

When my husband told me that he had joined an organization for crossdressers I was afraid for him to participate, and I really didn't want any part of it. I did not want to share our secret with anyone. It seemed too personal. I felt that we could be discovered. I did not want our friends to find out. There was the awareness that if career associates saw him dressed, our personal security would be in jeopardy. There were many unanswered questions and uncertainties that surrounded membership. Who are these people? Just how perverted are they? One wife told me that when she and her husband first joined she said, "OK. We will go, but I don't want any of these people to be our friends." She went on to say, "Now look what has happened. All of the people in the organization are our closest friends."

This is how it usually turns out. Crossdressers and their wives soon find out that other members share more common ground and more interest than any other group of people. We have gone on vacations with other members. We frequently go out socially with them. I have found that they are neither strange nor are they social misfits.

Frequently wives have concerns about the cost of membership. When we first joined there were many financial obligations. I was not sure just how much we could afford to invest in crossdressing. There were membership fees. Also we had to drive into Houston for meetings, stay in a hotel and eat out for the weekend. There were times that I would have preferred taking our money to Las Vagas or Reno.

It soon became apparent that the benefits were greater than the costs. We started to receive the FEMME MIRROR, a publication of TRI-ESS and THE FEMME FORUM, the monthly newsletter of the Houston TRI-ESS Chapter, TAU CHI. The articles helped us both during the adjustment stage and even now they represent a valuable addition to our library. We have also enjoyed and benefited from reading publications from other crossdressing organizations such as I.F.G.E. and Outreach.

SOME FAREWELL THOUGHTS FROM BETTY

Membership soon becomes a very vital part of the crossdresser's life. The realization of this is especially evident when members must move away. Betty is a crossdresser who was recently transferred to Washington state from Texas. She wrote the following farewell message to our group in Houston.

LOVELY, LOVELY TAU CHI SISTERS,

Parting company with friends and loved ones is always very difficult. But when one looks on the bright side you can always find many rays of sunshine. Through your energy and enthusiasm, you have given me a new confidence. Perhaps in the near future there will be an organization like TAU CHI in my new city. I am not very good with Greek, so you may be asked to help me again by suggesting a name for my new chapter that will honor TAU CHI of Houston. We should and hopefully will be sister organizations.

So these are not tears of sorrow. These are tears of joy, for you have given me the strength to be a leader too.

As I part I would like to leave you with a few of my more philosophical thoughts and a few quotes that have helped me.

Perhaps a little creed:

We are responsible when anyone reaches out for help

We want TRI-ESS to always be there.

And for this we will always be responsible

And don't forget.

There are no experts — only varying degrees of ignorance. This is so very true of us as crossdressers.

The future:

Worry about the future is very insane.

Why open the umbrella before it starts to rain?

The glory of tomorrow:

I would rather attempt something great and fail, than to attempt nothing at all and succeed! It is far better to dare to do mighty things, to win glorious triumphs, even though checkered with failure, than to rank with those poor spirits who neither enjoy much nor suffer much. They live in the gray twilight that knows not victory nor defeat.

UNITED WE STAND

I believe Betty will be leaving Houston a better person because she participated in TAU CHI. This is what membership in organizations is all about. We help each other grow as individuals. We will not all have the same theories about how life should be lived, but we share a common thread. To borrow an expression from American Express, "Membership has its privileges."

With the help of other members of the organization and the help of a supportive home environment, I believe the crossdresser can venture on into the quest of his own self-identity. I am committed to helping my husband. We will hold hands and venture out together. Life has brought us some challenges, but we have overcome them together. Life does not end with crossdressing. In many ways life expands toward new horizons.

EPILOGUE

This book has explored crossdressing, a subject that has never been clearly defined or understood. The causes have mystified researchers and the practice has broken families. The book has attempted to fill the voids by presenting this complex phenomenon from the vantage point of the wife. It has been created to provide factual information in an area of the behavioral sciences previously characterized by ignorance, fear, hostility and despair.

As the wife of a crossdresser I have moved from confusion to elation. The process that brought me to this point has been presented.

My hope is that the book will be received with an open mind. Things in life are seldom all good or bad; they are seldom all black or white. You will not agree with everything that was written. We each perceive things differently because our situations are different. Take the parts of the book that pertain to you and learn from it.

Human emotions are very real to the crossdresser. They have felt the painful rejection and loneliness that come when people do not understand them. They are probably one of the most misunderstood minorities in the world. This has intensified the painful experience of not being loved.

It does not need to be this way. Crossdressers are capable of being excellent husbands and fathers. Peace, joy and happiness can come to the crossdresser and his family once ignorance has been replaced with love. Reaching this point requires compromise from everyone including the crossdresser himself.

PS

To Melanie from Peggy,

IT IS OK IF YOU WANT TO WEAR MY CLOTHES!

GLOSSARY

CHROMOSOME PUSH . One theory used to explain the etiology of crossdressing by contending that the developing embryo is sexually undifferentiated for the first six weeks of the prenatal state. At that time the male Y chromosome pushes the gonads to develop the male genital tract, but in the case of crossdressers the push is weaker than it is in most males, thus there is the continuation of some female characteristics within the male psyche.

CONSTITUTIONAL FACTORS . One of several etiological explanations for transvestism. According to the constitutional theory transvestism is caused by biological factors.

CROSSDRESSER . A person who wears the clothing of the opposite gender. There are several million heterosexual, male crossdressers in the United States.

CROSSDRESSING . The act of wearing the clothing of the opposite gender. It has been estimated that there could be as high as 10% of the total male population who are involved in crossdressing.

DRAG QUEEN . A man who dresses in female clothing for the purpose of attracting other men sexually. Heterosexual crossdressers are not drag queens.

ENFEMME . Expressing female personality or wearing feminine clothing to express femininity. When enfemme the crossdresser wants to project feminine gender behavior.

ETIOLOGY . The science that assigns causes. The etiological causes of crossdressing are unclear, but there are numerous theories.

ETIOLOGIST . A person who studies causes. Etiologists attribute the need to crossdress to biological, environmental, or hormonal conditions, but these theories have not been proven.

FEMALE IMPERSONATOR . A man who develops his crossdressing into a performing art form. The actors who are female impersonators frequently leave the false impression that all crossdressers are either gay or sexually perverted.

FEMININITY. The doctrine favoring extension of the activities of women in social and political life; the qualities of females. The crossdresser wishes to personify his femininity.

FEMMOPHILE . A heterosexual male with a strong love of the feminine. The femmophile has a strong female component in his personality which is called the **femmeself**.

GENDER . Masculinity or femininity. Society has assigned a set of traits that are intended to distinguish the gender as either male or female.

GENDER CONTINUUM . A model showing gender traits on a continuum rather than as a dichotomy. The model presents gender traits clustering in four domains: positive masculine, negative masculine, positive feminine, and negative feminine. The new male image and the new female image of the eighties have been attributed to a more fluid movement within the domains.

GENDER DYSPHORIA . A condition characterized by restlessness, mental discomfort and general unhappiness with gender. Persons with a gender dysphoria may seek professional help.

GENETIC THEORY . One of several theories used to explain the etiology of transvestism. According to the genetic theory transvestism is inherited through the genes.

HETEROSEXUAL . Characterized by having sexual feelings for persons of the opposite sex. Male crossdressers are said to be heterosexual because they are attracted to women sexually.

HOMOSEXUAL . Characterized by having sexual feelings for persons of the same sex. The majority of male crossdressers are not homosexual.

MACHO . An especially virile, robust man. The heterosexual crossdresser attempts to break away from the macho stereotype.

NEW MAN\NEW WOMAN . A person who has had sexual reassignment surgery. Following surgery these people are referred to as a new man or new woman.

NEW FEMALE IMAGE . The idea that gender roles previously assigned to women are changing. Women are now assuming some roles previously assigned to men, thus the new female image has emerged.

NEW MALE IMAGE . The idea that gender roles are changing within society. The new male image permits a greater demonstration of female characteristics such as tenderness and a free expression of emotion.

PATERNAL THEORY . One of several theories used to explain the etiology of transvestism. According to this theory transvestism relates to the father's influence in the person's life. The paternal theory asserts that fathers of transvestites did not provide an adequate role model.

PRENATAL THEORY . Also called the symbiotic fusion. The prenatal theory attempts to explain transvestism by showing that there is a memory of existing with the mother prior to birth.

SECOND SELF . Recognizing the presence of both masculine and feminine traits within the personality. Crossdressers express their second self through feminine clothing and characteristics.

SEX . Refers to a person's chromosome pattern. A male is a person with an XY sex chromosome pattern; a female has an XX chromosome pattern.

SIGNIFICANT OTHER .(S.O.) A wife or a person other than the wife who has a meaningful, important relationship with the crossdresser. An understanding significant other can do much to help the crossdresser.

SYMBIOTIC FUSION . Also called the prenatal theory. According to the theory of symbiotic fusion, a prenatal memory of existing with the mother can explain the tendency for a man to become a crossdresser.

TRANSGENDERIST. A person who makes a permanent change in gender but does not have sexual reassignment surgery. Male crossdressers who are transgenderists live their entire life as women. Female transgenderists live their life as men.

TRANSSEXUAL . A person who has or is planning sexual reassignment surgery. A transsexual actually changes their sex from male to female or from female to male.

TRANSVESTITE. The practice of dressing in the clothing of the opposite sex. The word comes from Latin Trans (across) + Vestire (to clothe). Transvestite comedy has made Charlie's Aunt a durable commodity. Crossdressers are transvestites who dress for human fulfillment and not for laughs.

TV . A short form for the word, transvestite. The TV is usually a heterosexual crossdresser.

BIBLIOGRAPHY

Akerman, N. The Psychodynamics of Family Life. USA Books, Inc., 27. 1983.

Bader,A. Lousanne Psychiatrische Klinik Switzerland. "Observation on Modern Images." German Schweizer Archives fur Neurologic and Psychiatric. Vol. 119 {1} 49-72. 1976.

Bancroft, J. H., "The Relationship Between Gender Identity and Sexual Behavior: Some Clinical Aspects." In C. Ounsted & D. C. Taylor (Eds.), Gender Differences: Their Ontogeny and Significance. Edinburgh: Churchill Livingstone. 1972.

Bastani, J. B., Kentsmith, D. K., "Psychotherapy With Wives of Sexual Deviants." American Journal of Psychotherapy, 34, 20-25.

Benjamin, H., "Transvestism and Transsexualism." American Journal of Psychotherapy. 8, 219-230. 1954.

Bentler, P. M., & Prince, C., "Personality Characteristics of Male Transvestites." III. Journal of Abnormal Psychology. 74, 140-143. 1969.

Block, N. L. and Tessler, A. N., "Transsexuals and Surgical Procedures." Medical Aspects of Human Sexuality. Vol.7 {2} 158-186. 1973.

Branden, N., How to Raise Your Self Esteem. New York: Bantam Books. 1987.

Brierley, H., Transvestism: Illness, Perversion, or Choice. New York: Pergamon. 1979.

136

Brothers, J., "Ask Us." The Houston Post, June 3, 1982, Sec. 8B.

Brothers, J., "Ask Us." The Houston Post. May 1, 1981, Sec. 11D.

Buhrich, N. and McConaghy, N., Prince Henry Hospital Little Bay, Australia. "Transvestite Fiction." Journal of Nervous and Mental Disease. Vol. 163 {6} 420-27. Dec. 1973.

Buhrich. N. and McConaghy, N. St. Vincent Hospital, Darlig horst, Australia. "Parental Relationships During Childhood in Homosexuals, Transvestites, and Transsexuals." Journal of Psychiatry. Vol. 12 {2} 103-107. Jun, 1978.

Buhrich, N. and McConaghy, N. New South Wales Institute of Psychiatry, Leichhart, Australia. "Three Clinically Discrete Categories of Fetishistic Transvestism. Archives of Sexual Behavior. Vol. 8 {2} 151-157. March, 1979.

Buhrich, N., Theile, H., Yall, A., Crawford, A. St. Vincent Hospital, Darlinghurst, Australia. "Plasma Testosterone Serum FSH and Serum LH Levels in Transvestites." Archives of Sexual Behavior. Vol. 8 {1} 49-53. Jan. 1979.

Bullough, V. L., Bullough, B., and Smith, R. A., "Comparative Study of Male Transvestites, Male to Female Transsexuals, and Male Homosexuals." Journal of Sex Research, 19, 238-257. 1983.

Feinbloom, D., Transvestites and Transsexuals. New York: Delacort Press, 1963, p16.

Freund, K., Steiner, B. et al. "Two Types of Cross-Gender Identity." Archives of Sexual Behavior. 11, 49-63. 1982.

Goldfarb, J. H., "Concepts of Sexual Identity." Ph.D. Dissertation, University of Southern California. 1963.

Hirshfield, M., Die Transvestism. Berlin: Pulvermacher. 1987.

Kilgore, J., Executive Creative Director, Ogilvey and Mather, Houston, Texas. Telephone interview, 1983.

Koptagel, G., Istanbul University. Cerrahpasa Psychiatric Clinic. Confina Psychiatrica, Vol. 15 {1} 71-76. 1972.

Krueger, D.W., Baylor College of Medicine, Psychiatric Clinic of Houston, Texas. American Journal of Psychiatry. Vol. 135 {6} 739-742. June, 1978.

Laing, R. D., Self and Others. New York: Pantheon Books. 1969.

Lambley, P., University of Capetown S. Africa. "Treatment of Transvestism and Subsequent Coital Problems. Journal of Behavioral Therapy and Experimental Psychology. Vol. 5 {1} 101-102. July, 1974.

Langevin, R., "The Meaning of Cross-dressing." In B. Steiner (Ed.), Gender Dysphoria (pp.207-219). New York: Plenum Press. 1985.

Lukianowicz, N., "Survey of Various Aspects of Transvestism in Light of Our Present Knowledge." Journal of Nervous and Mental Disease. 129, 36-64. 1959.

Mac Kensie, K. R. U. Calgary School of Medicine. "Gender Dysphoria Syndron:Towards Standardardized Diagnostic Criteria." Archives of Sexual Behavior. Vol. 7 {4} 251-262 July. 1978.

Mead, M., Male and Female. New York: Mentor Press, 1955.

Meyer, J. K., John Hopkins Medical Institute Psychiatric Liaison Service. "Clinical Variants Among Applicants for Sex Reassignment." Archives of Sexual Behavior. Vol. 3 {6} 527-528. Nov, 1974.

Money, J. and Russo, A., John Hopkins University and Hospital. "Prepubertal Disorders of Gender Identity." Journal of Pediatric Psychology. Vol. 4 {1} 29-41. March, 1979.

Money, J., & Ehrhardt, A. A., Man and Woman, Boy and Girl. Baltimore: Johns Hopkins University Press. 1972.

Offit, Avodahk, The Sexual Self. New York: J. B. Lippincott Co. 1977.

Parens, H., Director of the Child Development Center, Eastern Penn. Psychiatric Institute, Philadelphia, Penn. Telephone Interview, October, 1982.

Person, E. and Ovesay, L., Columbia U. Coll. of Physicians and Surgeons. Psychoanalytical Clinic for Training and Research."The Transsexual Syndron in Males." American Journal of Psychotherapy. Vol. 28 {1} 174-193. April, 1974.

Person, E. and Oversey, L., Columbia U. Coll. of Physicians and Surgeons. "Transvestism: New Perspectives." Journal of American Academy of Psychoanalysis. Vol. 6 {3} 301-323. July, 1978.

Pietropinto, A. and Simernauer, J. Beyond the Male Myth, a National Survey. New York: New York Times Books. 1977.

Pomery, W., Cornell U. Medical School. "The Diagnosis and Treatment of Transvestites and Transsexuals." Journal of Sex and Marital Therapy. Vol. 1 {3} 215-224. Spring, 1975.

Prince, V., The Transvestite and His Wife. Los Angeles: Chevalier Publications. 1967.

Prince, V., How to be Woman Though Male. Los Angeles: Chevalier Publications. 1980.

Prince, V., Understanding Crossdressing. Los Angelos: Chevalier Publications. 1976.

Pugh, C., "Beyond the Male Myth." Houston Post, April 27, 1981, Sec. B1.

Ross, M. W., Rogers, L.J., McCulloch, H. U. Melbourne, Australia. "Stigma, Sex, and Society, A New Look at Gender Differentiation and Society." Journal of Homosexuality. Vol. 3, 315-330. Sum. 1978.

Shaw, G. B., Man and Superman. New York: Richard Mansfield, producer. 1903.

Simon, B., University of Houston Department of Sociology. Telephone interview, August 3, 1983.

Smith, R. W., California State University, Northridge, California. Sex Negative Society. 1981.

Stern, K. The Flight From Woman. New York: Farrar, Staus, andGiroux. 1965.

Stoller, R. J., Transsexuals and Transvestites. Los Angeles, The University of California Medical School Psychiatric Annuals. Vol.1 (4), 60-72. Dec.,1971.

Tanksley, P., Love Gift. Old Tappan, New Jersey: Fleming H. Revell Company. 1971.

Thorne, M., "LSD and Marital Therapy With a Transvestite and His Wife." Journal of Sex Research. 1967.

Walker, D. and Fletcher, P., Sex and Society.. New York: Pelican Books, 1984.

Whitley, R., Editor. "What's Your Definition of Femininity?" Glamour Magazine. Vol 75, #7, p.44. Spring, 1977.

Wise, T. N., "Coping With a Transvestite Mate : Clinical Implications." Journal of Sex and Marital Therapy. II: 293-300.

Wise, T. N., Meyer, J. K., "The Border Area Between Transvestism and Gender Dysphoria: Transvestite Applicants for Sex Reassignment." Archives of Sexual Behavior. 9, 327-342. 1980.

Wise, T. N., Dupkin, C. & Meyer, J. K., "Partners of Distressed Transvestites." American Journal of Psychiatry. 138, 1221-1224. 1981.

Zavitzianos, G., "Homeovestism: Perverse Form of Behavior." International Journal of Psycho-Analysis. Vol. 53, 471-477. 1972.

INDEX

acceptance
  by wives, 80-82
  of crossdressing, 61-66

beauty, 104

chromosome push, 131
clothing, ix
constitutional factors, 131
crossdresser
  acceptance of, 61-66, 113
  children of, 85-99
  definition of, ix, 5, 131
  erogenous zones, 60
  fear of rejection, 116
  fulfillment of, 107
  help by wife, 119-123
  intelligence of, 65
  love of femininity, 102-103
  macho behaviors, 101-102
  maternal instincts, 89-91
  need for beauty, 104
  need to share, 116
  parents of, 44-52, 50-51
  personality expression, 104-105
  professional help, 108-115
  rejection of, 114

144

definition of, 133

feminine avoidance, 37

marriage

courtship, 8-9

growth, 7-11

happiness, 7-11

masculine

gender expectations, 14-15

hormonal constitution, 49

life script, 20-21

negative factors, 37

positive factors, 37

masculinity, 37

men, 19-22

new female image, 13-14

new male image, 23-35

new man, 133

new woman, 133

parents of crossdressers

expectations of, 44-45

helping role of, 46-47

paternal theory, 133

questions asked by, 45-46

responsibility of, 52

personality, ix, x

phallic woman, 14

prenatal theory, 133

146

TRANSGENDER SUPPORT ORGANIZATIONS

Tri-Ess (The Society for the Second Self)
8880 Bellaire, B2, Suite 104
Houston, TX 77036
Email: JEFTRIS@aol.com
Web Site: http://www.tri-ess.org

IFGE (The International Foundation for Gender Education)
Box 229
Waltham, MA 02454-0229
(781) 899-2212
Email: ifge@ifge.org/
Web Site: http://www.ifge.org/

Renaissance
987 Old Eagle School
Wayne, PA 19087
Email: info@ren.org/
Web Site: http://www.ren.org/

SPICE (Spouses and Partner International Conference for Education)
PO Box 5304
Katy, TX 77491-5304
Email: desiree1@flash.net
Web Site: http://www.pmpub.com/spice.htm

Dignity Cruises (cruises for transgendered individuals and their significant others)
PO Box 5304
Katy, TX 77491-5304
Web Site: http://www.pmpub.com/cruise.htm

BOOKS PUBLISHED BY PM PUBLISHERS.

WHO'S REALLY FROM VENUS?: The Tale of Two Genders by Peggy J. Rudd, Ed.D. The author provides valuable suggestions on how to live life to the fullest through the integration of masculinity and femininity. ISBN 0-962676241. 5 1/2" x 8 1/2". 176 pages. Perfect bound paperback. 36 photos of transgendered individuals and significant people in their lives. $15.95 retail price.

CROSSDRESSERS: And Those Who Share Their Lives by Peggy J. Rudd, Ed.D. 51 photos and numerous true stories depict the transformation of men from the masculine to the feminine persona. Dr. Rudd carefully details strategies for coping, both for the crossdresser and those who share their lives. This book was featured on the Leeza Show on NBC. ISBN 0-9626762337. 5 1/2" x 8 1/2. 113 pages. Perfect bound paperback. $14.95 retail price.

CROSSDRESSING WITH DIGNITY: The Case for Transcending Gender Lines by Peggy J. Rudd, Ed.D. Is society ready for men who openly express femininity'? Can men transcend gender lines and maintain their sense of self-worth and dignity? These are questions asked to over 800 crossdressers in a survey used as the basis of this book. ISBN 0-962676268. 5 ½ x 8 1/2". 178 pages. Perfect bound paperback. $14.95 retail price

MY HUSBAND WEARS MY CLOTHES: Crossdressing from the Perspective of a Wife by Peggy J. Rudd, Ed.D. The first book on the unique topic of crossdressing written from the perspective of a wife. *"Clothes don't make the man",* has a new meaning. Dr, Rudd addresses many of the questions asked by the spouses, families and friends of men who crossdress. ISBN 0-96267625X. 5 1/2" x 8 1/2". 160 pages. Perfect bound paperback. $14.95 retail price.

LOVE CALENDAR: The Secrets of Love by Peggy J. Rudd, Ed.D. Dr. Rudd combines quotations with common sense applications. In this compassionate book, she encourages readers to spend five minutes daily in the *"Love Exercise."* **LOVE CALENDAR** is recommended for any couple seeking a happy, lasting relationship and those persons who are searching for love. ISBN 0-962676225. 5 1/2 x 8 1/2. 160 pages. Perfect bound paperback. $4.95 special price.

ORDER FORM MAY BE DUPLICATED

_____   **My Husband Wears My Clothes** $14.95

_____   **Who's Really From Venus?** $15.95

_____   **Crossdressers: And Those Who Share
Their Lives** $14.95

_____   **Crossdressing With Dignity** $14.95

_____   **Love Calendar: The Secrets of Love** $4.95

_____   Sub-total

_____   20% Discount or 30% discount 3 or more books

_____   Sales tax - Texas residents add 08%

_____   Shipping 10% of total order domestic or 15% of
total order for international. For air mail
international add $2.00 each book

_____   Total

You may pay by check, money order or credit card:

Credit Cards: ( ) Visa ( ) Mastercard ( ) Discover ( ) AX

_____   _____
. Credit Card Number   Exp. Date

_____
Name On Card

_____
Street   City   State   Zip Code

_____   _____
Signature   Email

Mail or fax to:

PM Publishers
P.O. Box 5304
Katy, TX 77491-5304
Fax: (281) 347-8747
Email: pmpub@pmpub.com
Secure ordering at: http://www.pmpub.com/books.htm

ORDER FORM MAY BE DUPLICATED

_____ **My Husband Wears My Clothes** $14.95

_____ **Who's Really From Venus?** $15.95

_____ **Crossdressers: And Those Who Share Their Lives** $14.95

_____ **Crossdressing With Dignity** $14.95

_____ **Love Calendar: The Secrets of Love** $4.95

_____ Sub-total

_____ 20% Discount or 30% discount 3 or more books

_____ Sales tax - Texas residents add 08%

_____ Shipping 10% of total order domestic or 15% of total order for international. For air mail international add $2.00 each book

_____ Total

You may pay by check, money order or credit card:

Credit Cards: ( ) Visa ( ) Mastercard ( ) Discover ( ) AX

_____   _____
Credit Card Number   Exp. Date

_____
Name On Card

_____
Street   City   State   Zip Code

_____   _____
Signature   Email

Mail or fax to:

PM Publishers
P.O. Box 5304
Katy, TX 77491-5304
Fax: (281) 347-8747
Email: pmpub@pmpub.com
Secure ordering at: http://www.pmpub.com/books.htm

ORDER FORM MAY BE DUPLICATED

———— **My Husband Wears My Clothes** $14.95

———— **Who's Really From Venus?** $15.95

———— **Crossdressers: And Those Who Share Their Lives** $14.95

———— **Crossdressing With Dignity** $14.95

———— **Love Calendar: The Secrets of Love** $4.95

———— Sub-total

———— 20% Discount or 30% discount 3 or more books

———— Sales tax - Texas residents add 08%

———— Shipping 10% of total order domestic or 15% of total order for international. For air mail international add $2.00 each book

———— Total

You may pay by check, money order or credit card:

Credit Cards: ( ) Visa ( ) Mastercard ( ) Discover ( ) AX

————————————————   ————————
Credit Card Number   Exp. Date

————————————————
Name On Card

————————————————————————————
Street   City   State   Zip Code

————————————————   ————————————————
Signature   Email

Mai! or fax to:

PM Publishers
P.O. Box 5304
Katy, TX 77491-5304
Fax: (281) 347-8747
Email: pmpub@pmpub.com
Secure ordering at: http://www.pmpub.com/books.htm